Clive E[xton]

Barking i[n Essex]

Clive Exton was born in London in 1930 and grew up in Islington. After training as an actor at Central School, his first two plays were produced by ITV in 1959. He wrote eight plays for 'Armchair Theatre' from 1960 to 1964. *The Trial of Dr Fancy* was one of the earliest cases of censorship in commercial television, delayed for two years by the ITA on the basis that it might cause offence. *The Big Eat* (1962) was turned down by ITV as it was an attack on advertising and was produced by the BBC in 1965. For the BBC he co-wrote *The Boundary* with Tom Stoppard and *The Rainbirds* (Play for Today) both 1971. Feature films included *No Place to Go* (1963), *Night Must Fall*, directed by Karel Reisz (1964), *Entertaining Mr Sloane* (1970) and *10 Rillington Place* (1971). A collaboration with Brian Eastman produced four series of *Jeeves and Wooster* (for which Clive received the Writers' Guild Award), many episodes of *Poirot* and *Rosemary & Thyme*. *Barking in Essex* follows plays including *Have You Any Dirty Washing, Mother Dear?* (Hampstead, 1971), *Twixt* (produced throughout France, Italy and Germany) and *Murder is Easy* (Duke of York's, 1993). Clive died in 2007 at the age of seventy-seven.

Clive Exton

Barking in Essex

B L O O M S B U R Y
LONDON • NEW DELHI • NEW YORK • SYDNEY

Bloomsbury Methuen Drama

An imprint of Bloomsbury Publishing Plc

50 Bedford Square   1385 Broadway
London   New York
WC1B 3DP   NY 10018
UK   USA

www.bloomsbury.com

Bloomsbury is a registered trade mark of Bloomsbury Publishing Plc

First published 2013
Reprinted 2013

© Estate of Clive Exton, 2013

Clive Exton has asserted his rights under
the Copyright, Designs and Patents Act 1988
to be identified as the Author of this work

British Library Cataloguing-in-Publication Data
A catalogue record for this book is available from the British Library.

ISBN: PB: 978-1-4725-2455-3
ePDF: 978-1-4725-2315-0
ePub: 978-1-4725-3414-9

Library of Congress Cataloging-in-Publication Data
A catalog record for this book is available from the Library of Congress.

Typeset by Country Setting, Kingsdown, Kent CT14 8ES
Printed and bound in Great Britain

Barking in Essex

Barking in Essex was first presented in London on 6 September 2013 at the Wyndham's Theatre, where it was produced by MJE Productions, Theatre Royal Haymarket Productions and James Quaife Productions. The cast was as follows:

Darnley Packer	Lee Evans
Emmie Packer	Sheila Hancock
Chrissie Packer	Keeley Hawes
Rocco Dimaggio	Karl Johnson
Allegra Tennyson	Montserrat Lombard

Directed by Harry Burton
Designed by Simon Higlett
Lighting by James Farncombe
Sound by Gareth Owen
Casting by Anne Vosser

Characters

Darnley Packer, *mid-thirties*
Emmie Packer, *Darnley's mother, fifties*
Chrissie Packer, *Darnley's wife, early thirties*
Rocco Dimaggio, *a hit man, seventy-five*
Allegra Tennyson, *a barrister's junior, thirty-five*

Act One

It is early on a bright summer's morning. The large and expensively furnished sitting room of the Packers' house in suburban Essex is empty. The house having been built in the 1960s, there is an open-tread staircase to the upper floors and an archway leading to the hall. On the other side of the hall we can see the swing door into the kitchen.

A woman's angry voice shouts from somewhere out of sight in the hall.

Chrissie (*offstage*)   You cunt!

There is no reply to this except for the slamming of a door.

After a moment, **Chrissie Packer***, a pretty, well-dressed woman in her early thirties, strides in from the hall. She hurls her handbag on to the white leather sofa and stands for a moment, fuming. She then goes back to the archway and shouts:*

Chrissie   You cunt!

We see legs descending the staircase. They belong to **Emmie Packer***.* **Emmie** *is some fifty years old, blonde and well presented. She wears trainers, and a pretty dressing gown over her nightdress.*

Emmie   Here, here, here, here, here!

Chrissie   What?

Emmie   Who are you calling a cunt?

Chrissie   Your precious Darnley.

Emmie   Oh, don't call him that, love – you're happily married. What's he done now?

Chrissie   Did you see him last night?

Emmie   No! He weren't on! I sat up to watch the fucking thing and –

Chrissie   They cut him out, that's why!

Emmie   How do you mean?

Chrissie   They do it on film before.

Emmie   He weren't on. I watched it.

Chrissie   He done it and they cut him out!

Emmie, *not understanding, looks at her in frustration.*

Emmie   Where is he now, then?

Chrissie   In the lav. He got a kick there last night.

Emmie   Where?

Chrissie   At the studio.

Emmie   No, I mean whereabouts on the like . . .

Chrissie   Oh! In the . . .

Emmie   Goolies?

Chrissie   Yeah. Well – nearby.

Emmie   Where was he last night? After they cut him out, like?

Chrissie   He weren't nowhere! What are you talking about? They wouldn't even let us stay on at the hotel, even.

Emmie   No!

Chrissie   Stood over us while we packed.

Emmie   They never did!

Chrissie   And they call this a free fucking country!

Emmie   I know.

Chrissie   Standing there in their stupid buttons and them bits of rope on their shoulders . . . ! Little tin-pots, they think they are.

Emmie   Cunts. Who?

Chrissie   These so-called security guards! Cunts.

Chrissie *goes to her bag, gets out a cigarette and lights it.* **Emmie** *watches her.*

Emmie   So what, like, happened, then? What about the money?

Chrissie   There isn't any fucking money!

Emmie   What? Nothing?

Chrissie   Nothing!

Emmie   Oh, shit! Oh, Chrissie! Oh, shit! What are we going to do?

Chrissie   I don't know. Christ!

Emmie   He was our only chance!

Chrissie   Fat chance, him!

Emmie   Will you tell us what happened!

Chrissie   Doesn't fucking matter, does it? Listen. He did the Fastest Finger First, right?

Emmie   Right.

Chrissie   Six point four seconds.

Emmie   What was the question?

Chrissie   Some rubbish. Anyhow, up he gets and Chris Tarrant puts his arm round him . . .

Emmie   He's nice, isn't he?

Chrissie   He had it in for Darnley.

Emmie   No!

Chrissie   He fucking did!

Darnley Packer *has appeared in the archway. He is in his mid-thirties.*

Darnley   It's coming out all blood.

Chrissie   Serve you fucking right.

Darnley   Sort of lumps, too.

Emmie   What have they done to you, son?

Darnley   I got a sort of kick, Mum. In the goolies.

Emmie   They don't usually do that, do they?

Chrissie   They don't usually have a complete cunt there.

Emmie   Oh, they do!

Darnley   What happened was –

Chrissie   I've told her.

Darnley   – they had Fastest Finger First and I did C-A-B-D, like we agreed, but it were wrong and I just had to sit there while this personal executive assistant from up north somewhere won sixty-four thousand pounds.

Chrissie   Get on with it, if you're going to!

Darnley   Well, when she'd finished we did Fastest Finger again C-A-B-D – and this time it come out right.

Emmie   What was the question?

Darnley   I don't know, I never got to the end of it. Just got straight in there – C-A-B-D. Boof! Yess!

He holds his clenched fists aloft.

So I get up and – you know that sort of like slow-motion run I do? I do that all the way over to Chris Tarrant. They loved that! What? Laughing! Clapping! 'Ray! Anyway, Chris is grinning all over and he puts his arm round me and without moving his lips he says, 'Cut it out.' I was getting the limelight, see. They don't like that. What he didn't know was that I can do that ventriloquist stuff, and all. Remember that show I used to put on with old Algie? So, all smiles, I say, 'Piss off, you Brummagen cunt'! You try saying that without moving your lips! I tell you what – he went white! I could feel him digging his fingers into my arm. I've got a bruise there, haven't I, Chrissie?

Chrissie   Oh, do leave it out, Darnley.

Darnley   Chris Tarrant's finger-marks all down my triceps. That must be worth a bit. *Hello* magazine would pay big bucks for a picture of that.

Chrissie   Get on with it!

Emmie   So what happened? Why didn't you win the money?

Darnley   It were all fixed, Mum.

Chrissie   Tell her about the reading. You want to make a complete cunt of yourself? Tell her about the reading.

Darnley   What reading?

Chrissie (*to* **Emmie**)   You know when Tarrant smarms them up before he asks them the questions? 'What are you going to do with the money?' 'What are your hobbies?'

Emmie   How much money will make a difference? Duh. A million quid, dickhead!

She laughs.

Chrissie   Well, cunt-face here tells Chris his hobby is reading!

Emmie   Reading? What's he like, eh? He wouldn't know a book if it bit him in the bollocks!

Darnley   No – but they like that! Watch the programme! That's all I'll say – watch the programme. Them people who says things like they like reading books – they always win the most money.

Emmie   It's true, you know. I never thought of that.

Darnley   People with posh accents, they win a lot, and all. 'Oh, good evening, Chris. I likes readin' books and playin' polo.' I practised that, but I lost my nerve. I thought it might interfere with my like concentration.

Chrissie   So, of course, the first question they ask him is one of these literally ones, isn't it?

Emmie   How do you mean?

Chrissie   First question, right? A hundred quid. 'What animals was it that Little Bo-Peep had lost? Was it, A, her dogs; B, her cats; C, her sheep; or D, her – what was it?

Darnley   Oh – some fucking thing.

Chrissie   Her dinosaurs!

Emmie *laughs.*

Chrissie   You know what the cunt says?

Emmie   No. Go on.

Chrissie   Dog. He says dog! Duh!

Darnley   I thought that's what it was!

Chrissie   Dog!

Darnley   How was I meant to know?

Chrissie   Little Bo-Peep has lost her dogs! 'Final answer, Darnley?' 'Final answer, Chris.'

Darnley   I thought it were a trick question! There was that thing in the paper – oh, ages ago – about how Chris Tarrant had lost his dog. Offering a reward and everything.

Chrissie   How is Chris Tarrant Little Bo-Peep all of a sudden?

Darnley   How was I to know? They get you all confused! Lights going up and down, music going off and on, him sitting there taking the piss . . .

Chrissie   I'm ashamed to be married to you, Darnley Packer. He don't even know a simple nursery rhyme!

Darnley   I'm not a fucking kid, am I? Why should I know a fucking nursery rhyme?

Chrissie   Because it's part of your heritage, innit? Because you've been blessed with the language of Shakespeare, you cunt!

Emmie   Oh, I hate Shakespeare! All them thees and thous and talking like a cunt. 'I wandered lonely as a cloud . . . ' I'd give him fucking wander. I'd wander him right up the jacksie with a sharp stick. Making little kids learn all that rubbish! Kids ought to be out enjoying theirselves. Time enough for learning a lot of miserable rubbish when you're my age.

Darnley (to **Chrissie**)   What do you know about Shakespeare, anyhow? You won't even let me watch that thing about doctors cutting people up to see what they died of!

Chrissie   What's that got to do with Shakespeare?

Darnley   It's all culture, innit? You learn a lot from programmes like that. There was this bloke walked around fourteen years with a bullet in his brain. Or was it his heart? I know it was somewhere.

Chrissie   Oh, you learned a fucking lot from that, didn't you?

Darnley   Well, you say us some Shakespeare, then. You're such a expert all of a sudden – recite us some Shakespeare.

Chrissie   Why should I? Ignorant cunt.

Darnley   You don't know none, that's why! She don't know none!

Chrissie   What about 'To be or not to be . . . '? That's Shakespeare.

Darnley   'To be or not to be . . . '! What's that supposed to mean, then?

Chrissie   Don't matter what it means – it's like in the words like.

Emmie   The clue's in the question.

Chrissie   Anyway, I didn't say I was a expert. *Romeo and Juliet*!

Darnley   What do you mean, *Romeo and Juliet*?

Chrissie   That's Shakespeare!

Darnley   You can't just say words and say, 'That's Shakespeare'!

Emmie   You're taking advantage, Chrissie, you are. Darnley didn't go to university like you did.

Chrissie   We didn't do Shakespeare, not in Media Studies.

Emmie   I hate Shakespeare.

Chrissie   He wrote plays and that. We did one at school, one Christmas. I played Mary Mandolin.

Emmie   You know who I blame? I blame the teachers. Who do they think they are, anyway? Standing out in the front, telling you what to do. I never let them tell my boys nothing, did I, Darn?

Darnley   You remember old McGarrity? The bald git you duffed up?

Chrissie   They try to tell you what to wear, and all! This Mary Mandolin was on the game, apparently, and I –

Emmie   Can we get back to the matter in hand? We're not here to discuss fucking Shakespeare. I want to know what happened last night, not five thousand fucking years ago. Darnley didn't know Little Bo-Peep. So that was it, was it?

Chrissie   No! That was just the start of it! 'Give him a big hand,' says Tarrant. So, here, what do you think cuntox here does? He grabs hold of Chris Tarrant!

Emmie   No!

Chrissie   He does!

Darnley   'I'll fucking give you a big hand', I says! Boof!

Emmie   Good for you, boy!

Chrissie   Drags him off his stool, across that computer thing and really lays into him.

Darnley   Well – he were having a laugh, wasn't he? 'I'll fucking give you a big hand!' Boof!

Chrissie   So these four security guards appear from like nowhere and starts dragging cunt-features away.

Darnley   And that bugger with the headphones.

Emmie   I never could stand that Chris Tarrant. What sort of name is that? Tarrant! Tarantula, more like. Here! Chris Tarantula! Slimy git. Good for you, Darnley!

Darnley   No, he was out of order. I've nothing against the man, as such, but he was well out of order, doing me a question like that just because I'd done my slow-motion run.

He demonstrates.

Clapping and cheering! Hooray! They really loved it.

Emmie   Tarrant was well out of order, son. No doubt about that.

Chrissie   Never mind about out of order – what are we going to do about the money?

Darnley   That's my one regret.

Emmie   You got nothing to reproach yourself for, Darnley. He was out of order.

Darnley   No, but I thought we'd be well away for the money, like. I knew you was a bit skint.

Emmie   You done your best, son. Nobody can't do more.

Darnley   It just come to me, like. I just woke up like thinking 'Who wants to be a millionaire?' Like a voice in my head. Calling, calling . . . Then it clicked. I thought – I fucking do, I thought! So I phoned.

Emmie   Didn't they call in like the Old Bill?

Chrissie   No!

Darnley   They talked about it, but . . .

Chrissie   They're all fucking talk.

Emmie   They can talk the talk, but can they walk the walk?

Chrissie   They don't want the publicity, do they? They work in the shadows, these people.

Darnley   They knew Tarrant was out of order. I mean, the way he sat there grinning. You know what I mean?

Emmie   He's evil, that man – evil! I'm going to phone Rocco.

Chrissie   Who's Rocco?

Emmie *takes her mobile out of her dressing-gown pocket.*

Darnley   No, Mum – don't! He's not worth it. I'll get him myself one day, don't you fret. Rocco don't do celebrities, anyway.

Emmie   Get out of it! He done Monty Brackenbury!

Darnley   Monty weren't a celebrity, Mum. He just had a celebrity lifestyle – cocaine and dodgy hair-dos and that. Monty were one of us – he'd done more bird than Bernard Matthews at Christmas. And, anyway, Monty weren't a contract, not as such. Rocco only done him because he'd put Rocco's granddaughter up the duff at her mum's funeral. Taking advantage of her grief like.

Emmie   Funerals can affect you like that, though. Mind you, Edwina always banged like a shit-house door, funeral or not. If you're that way disposed of you have to fit it in where you can.

Darnley   Edwina fitted it in all right!

Emmie   Darnley!

Darnley   Sorry, Mum.

Emmie   Tell you what, though – you should try on that other one.

Darnley   What other one?

Emmie   You know – with old sourpuss.

Darnley   Oh – 'The Leakiest Wank'.

Emmie   Yeah – have a go at that.

Darnley   Nah. The money's peanuts on that. Anyway, I don't know as I'd be at my best in a competitive environment.

Emmie   You could give that Annie Robinson a good kicking!

Darnley   Yeah! Catch! Boof!

Chrissie *speaks very slowly and emphatically, forcing them to listen.*

Chrissie   Algie is sitting on the train now. They let him out at eight o'clock and now he's on the train. He's coming here.

Emmie *stares at her for a moment, then turns and hurries towards the stairs.*

Emmie   I'm going to finish packing.

Darnley   Packing?

Emmie   If you think I'm going to be here when Algie arrives, you've got another think coming. I got my passport out ready last night.

Darnley   Passport? What are we talking about here?

Chrissie   Money.

Darnley   She don't have to worry about money no more. Algie's got money. He worked hard for it, Algie did. He's done his time, he's paid his debt to society. Now he's got a right to sit back and enjoy the fruits of his labour. That's what democracy means.

Emmie   Oh, I can't be doing with this!

She heads for the stairs again.

Chrissie   It's no good running away, Emmie. He'll only come after you.

Emmie   I'm his mother!

Chrissie   All the more reason. He put his trust in you.

Darnley   Is something wrong?

Chrissie (*to* **Emmie**)   You tell him.

Emmie   I can't!

Chrissie   He's got to know sooner or later.

Emmie *gathers herself.*

Emmie   Darnley.

Darnley   Yes, Mum?

Emmie   I'm your mother, ain't I?

Darnley   Yes, Mum.

Emmie   I wouldn't never deceive you, would I?

Darnley *thinks hard.*

Emmie   You don't have to fucking think about it!

Darnley   Well, you did tell me Dad was my dad.

Emmie   That was a white lie, son. A harmless little white lie. It wasn't meant to deceive no one. It was more for your father's peace of mind, God rest his soul. And to keep him from doing his pieces.

Chrissie   I didn't know about this! Who was his dad, then?

Emmie   Best not to say, isn't it? Not at this junction.

Darnley   She's not sure.

Emmie   All right! All right! I done wrong, I admit it. I was young. I was impressionable. Your father was busy building up the scrap business . . .

Chrissie   Was it someone we know?

Emmie   I'd rather not say.

Chrissie   It was someone we know! Who was it, Darn?

Darnley   How should I know? She'd never tell me.

Emmie   I'll only say this – I wouldn't portray the boys' father with some stranger. It were one of his partners.

Chrissie and **Darnley** *both stare at* **Emmie**.

Chrissie   But he only ever had one partner.

Emmie   No he didn't. He had the Winker, early on.

Chrissie   The Winker? He only had one eye and a whelk!

Emmie   I always thought he was rather attractive. Course he was younger then. But it wasn't him, anyway.

Chrissie   But his only other partner was my dad!

Emmie   Oh, yes.

Chrissie   You don't mean to say you and Dad . . .

Emmie   It was a moment's folly, Chrissie, that's all. He was a romantic devil, your father – hung like a drayman's horse. He come into the yard one day when Chazz was out on the rob. I was down there doing the books in them days. This was when we was still in Barking. He wooed me. I mean, men just can't be bothered these days, can they? And don't think I didn't put up a fight! But he was so kind and gentle and I'd heard about the size of him from your mother, so . . . I mean, she used to complain about it! I used to say to her, 'If that's the only thing you've got to complain about, girl . . . '
Anyhow, in ten minutes he had me bent over the bonnet of an old Vauxhall Victor and was rogering me speechless.

Darnley   I don't know as I want to hear this, Mum.

Emmie   No, it's nice! You've got no romance in your soul, Darnley, that's your trouble. He was down there every morning after that. After dinner sometimes, and all. I'll never forget that Vauxhall Victor. Lovely sort of maroon colour, it was. I used to think it was Welsh.

Chrissie   Welsh?

Emmie   From where I was I could see all the way through to the rear window and it had this notice in the back – 'TAELGNOL TA SNOIL EHT NEES EVEW'.

Chrissie   What does that mean?

Emmie   It was only later in the week when I saw it from the other side – 'WE'VE SEEN THE LIONS AT LONGLEAT'. Happy days, happy days.

She stands for a moment, lost in a golden reverie.

Darnley   Mum?

Emmie   What, darling?

Darnley   That don't prove nothing. It could still have been Dad was my father.

Emmie   No, son. He was still wrestling in them days and he was in training. You know what he was like when he was in training. He wouldn't look at it, little own touch it. It was like being married to the Pope, or something. I told him. I said, 'You ought to get one of them big hats.' I mean, weeks on end sometimes! A woman needs them little things – flowers, chocolates, getting up in the morning feeling bow-legged. 'My body's a temple', he used to say. 'Oh, yes?' I'd say, 'Well, mine's King's Cross Station but we ain't had a bleeding train in there for a fortnight.'

Chrissie   Wait a minute, wait a minute! It's my father we're talking about here.

Emmie   No – this was Chazz. My husband.

Chrissie   No, but before. The Vauxhall Victor and that. My dad wasn't like that. He was a highly religious man, my dad was. He used to read us bits out the *Reader's Digest*. The whole family had to go to church regular, every Christmas. He didn't hold with Easter.

Darnley   Why not?

Chrissie   He said it was more like foreign. He couldn't stand nothing foreign. He wouldn't have chips, even, if they called them French fries. He was always interested in politics.

Darnley   But don't this mean Chrissie's my sister?

Emmie (*regretfully*)   No! Only half-sister.

Chrissie   But we're married!

Emmie   I know – it's lovely, isn't it? Half-sister, half-wife. I think that's lovely.

Chrissie   Never mind about lovely! It's fucking illegal!

Emmie   Don't you worry, Chrissie. If the busys come round sticking their nose in, I'll deny every word of it.

Chrissie   They can do tests!

Darnley   Leaving aside the legal prospects – there's the other stuff – the scientific stuff – genes and all.

Emmie   Oh, these so-called scientists! What do they know! One minute they tell you you've got to eat bread and stuff and the next minute bread's next door to poison. Sending men up the moon and that and they can't run the buses on time. I can't be doing with science.

Chrissie   But we want to have children!

Emmie   It'll be lovely! They can call you Mum and Dad or Uncle and Auntie. It's good for a child to have freedom like that.

Darnley (*to* **Chrissie**)   She's got a point, you know.

Chrissie   We should of been told. I mean, I've been living a lie, haven't I? I mean, without even fucking knowing it! It's disgusting! It's like saying the only man I could get was my own brother!

Darnley   No, but I quite like it – Sis.

He puts his arm round her.

Chrissie   You don't, do you?

Darnley   I do! It's nice. I mean, it's double-bubble, innit? Two for the price of one, like.

Chrissie *smiles up at him.*

Chrissie   Oh, go on, then.

Darnley   I don't half fancy you – Sis.

Chrissie   You're just saying that.

Emmie   There you are, you see? It'll be nice to have a big brother to look after you. Keep it all in the family, like.

Darnley *suddenly doubles over with pain, clutching at his groin.*

Darnley   Oh, I got to go! Oh, it don't half hurt!

Doubled over, he hurries off to the lavatory.

Chrissie   You still haven't told him about the money!

Emmie   Oh, I can't, Chrissie.

Chrissie   You haven't got any choice!

Emmie   We could just leave.

Chrissie   What, just leave Darnley to face Algie?

A strangled cry of pain comes from the direction of the lavatory.

Emmie   Oh, he's such a baby!

Chrissie   We can't just leave him!

Emmie   Well, you stay behind if you like, girl.

Chrissie   You've got to tell him!

Darnley *comes back into the room.*

Darnley   It's worse than ever now. It's not just like a mixture, it's all blood. And even more lumps than before. Great black lumps.

Emmie   We don't want all the gory details, thank you very much.

Darnley   I can't have caught something, can I?

Emmie   Yeah, you caught a boot in the bollocks.

She laughs.

Darnley   Only the whole of my whatsit's swollen now.

Chrissie   That makes a change.

Darnley   Here, I've been thinking, though. About what you said about you and Chrissie's dad. What about Algie?

Emmie   Oh, no! He come after the wrestling. Chazz only took up the wrestling because he was creative, see, and he was like looking for an outlet. When he got properly into blagging he was all right. I mean, he didn't have to go on treating his body like a temple and that.

Darnley   No, but am I still related to him? To Algie? I can't work it out.

Emmie   Course you are! He's still your brother, isn't he? Just like he was before.

Chrissie   What about me?

Emmie   What, you and Algie? Well, he's still your brother-in-law, but now he's your half-brother and all. Or is it half-stepbrother? And I'm your auntie, I think.

Chrissie   As well as my mother-in-law?

Emmie   Uh – yes. That's right.

Darnley   Here – what's the time?

He looks at his watch.

Oh, shit! It's ten past ten! I got to go and sign on!

Chrissie   You can't go and sign on!

Darnley   I'll lose my benefit.

Chrissie   Never mind about your benefit. She was telling you something important.

Darnley   Can't it wait?

Emmie   Course it can, darling.

Chrissie   No, it fucking can't.

Emmie   Oh. Well, it's like this, Darnley. I mean, you know Algie done that safe deposit job?

Darnley   Course I know! That's what he got the seven years for! He'd of got fifteen if they'd found the gun.

Emmie   And you know his share of the job was three million quid?

Darnley   Three million, six hundred and seventy-two thousand.

Emmie   All right, all right! What are you – some sort of bleeding accountant all of a sudden?

Darnley   In untraceable notes! Yess! Result! Here – you remember that post office I did?

Emmie   Well – it's ironic, really.

Chrissie   It is! Dead ironic!

Darnley   Over in Royston. Eight thousand pounds they had there.

Chrissie   We don't want to hear about it, Darnley!

Darnley   No, but I'm just saying –

Chrissie   Just listen, will you?

Emmie   Well, I mean, you have to laugh, I suppose. All that loot, he put it in a safe deposit box.

Darnley   It's never been done over!

Emmie   No! No, no, no, no, no. Course it ain't. They made them places more secure after Algie done that one. They was a disgrace before. That's what give him the idea. It was their own fault, if you ask me, leaving temptation lying in the way of an ambitious man like your brother.

Chrissie   They had no right.

Emmie   They're the ones who ought to of done the time! I'd have no mercy on people like that.

Darnley   Well, what's the trouble, then?

Emmie   Well, Chrissie and me –

Chrissie   Here! You can leave me out of it!

Emmie   Oh, yes?

Darnley   Out of what?

Emmie   Well – Chrissie and me we like dipped into it a bit.

Darnley *stares at her.*

Darnley   Into the money?

Emmie   Well – yes. Sort of. You know.

Darnley (*slowly*)   You shouldn't of done that, Mum.

Emmie   I know. I know. It were wrong. I feel ever so bad about it, son. But times was hard, and you know how it is – you think – well, I'll just borrow a couple of quid and put it back next week when I get my giro.

Darnley   Well – not too much harm done, I suppose.

Emmie   Oh, no. It was his own fault, leaving the key lying around, really.

Darnley   I thought he give it you for safe keeping.

Emmie   Well – in a way, yes.

Darnley   What do you mean – in a way? I mean, I were there, weren't I? He said, 'You keep this, Mum, for safe keeping.'

Emmie   He did say that, yes.

Chrissie   He give her the password, and all.

Emmie   Oh, thanks a lot, Chrissie.

Chrissie   In case anything happened to him.

Darnley   He put his trust in you, Mum. You wouldn't portray that trust.

Emmie   No, I wouldn't. I didn't. Well, not very much I didn't.

Darnley   I mean – how much?

Emmie   How much what?

Darnley   How much did you like dip in?

Emmie   Oh . . .

Darnley   I mean, there's plenty left for Algie?

Emmie   Oh . . .

Darnley   How much? How much is left?

Emmie   I couldn't say, exactly. Not exactly, I couldn't. I haven't like done the figures.

Chrissie   Fifty-five.

Darnley   Fifty-five?

Chrissie   Fifty-five.

Darnley (*incredulously*)   Fifty-five thousand pounds!

Chrissie   Well – no.

Darnley   What do you mean, 'no'?

Chrissie   Not fifty-five thousand.

Emmie   Fifty-five pounds.

Darnley *stares at her, disbelievingly.*

Emmie   It could of been much worse. We thought it was only five, didn't we, Chrissie?

Chrissie   We found a fifty had slipped down the side of the box.

Emmie   It's got a sort of metal lining, the box, and it had slipped down in there. It's a silly way to make them, really. I'm going to complain about it next time I'm −

Darnley *manages to find his voice.*

Darnley   You mean you've spent three million, six hundred and seventy-one thousand, nine hundred and forty-five pounds?

Emmie   Well, like I say, I haven't like done the figures, yet.

Chrissie   It's been five years, nearly!

Darnley   I know how long it's been. That's about seven hundred thousand pounds a year.

Emmie   He's ever so good at figures, ain't he, Chrissie?

Darnley   That's fifteen thousand pounds a week!

Emmie   It don't go nowhere these days! Have you seen the price of things in the shops? Them sausages you had Tuesday for dinner − two pounds seventy a pound, they cost! For sausages! You men, you just don't know, do you? If you had to do the shopping, we'd soon hear a different story.

Darnley   You could pave the whole country ankle-deep in sausages for that money! And still have enough left over to cover Wales in mash!

Emmie   Good thing, too, I'd say. You remember that Welsh milkman we had? I'm sure he was on the fiddle. He used to −

Darnley   He'll kill you.

Chrissie   If he kills us, he's got to kill you, and all.

Darnley   Why me? I didn't spend his money.

Chrissie   What about them Ferraris?

Darnley   What?

Chrissie   Them two Ferraris you bought.

Darnley   Are you saying that were my fault? The first one was rubbish! Who ever heard of a powder-blue Ferrari?

Emmie   What did you buy it for, then?

Darnley   I didn't buy it! They made me! They did this big like sales spiel on me – said it was like the only one they had – if I didn't take it I'd have to wait six weeks . . . I was like – What? As soon as I got it home, I realised. Anyway, that money was from a win you had on the horses, you said.

Emmie   Horses! Do you think the horses paid for that world cruise I give you for your anniversary?

Darnley   That were nice, that cruise. (*To* **Chrissie**.) You remember in Hong Kong or somewhere – them natives jabbering away like monkeys?

Chrissie   That were Rio de Janerio.

Darnley   It were educational, that.

Emmie   So it fucking ought to be for a hundred and twelve thousand quid! Of your brother's money!

Darnley   No! You said you'd won it down Tesco's! You know, the holiday of a lifetime if you buy three packets of Pringles. Oh, shit!

Chrissie   Look – if we just tell Algie . . .

Darnley   He'll kill us.

Chrissie   No – if we like sit him down – give him a drink – explain it to him.

Darnley   Slowly and painfully, he'll kill us.

Emmie   No! I will not have that, Darnley. Algie is not a cruel man.

Darnley   What do you mean, he's not a cruel man? I mean, Algie's my little brother. He's my mate. My prodigy, you might say. But you can't deny he's got a cruel streak. He cut off one of Uncle Arthur's thumbs that Christmas! Then the day after Boxing Day he cut off the other one!

Emmie   Well, Arthur had annoyed him.

Darnley   All he said was he didn't like the stuffing!

Emmie   It wasn't just that.

Darnley   Yes, it was! Arthur said, 'This stuffing's a bit pony, innit?'

Emmie   It wasn't just that.

Darnley   Algie pinned his hand to the table with the carving fork. Boof!

Emmie   He's excitable! Arthur had been bitching about the hospitality ever since he got here. Getting at me, is what he was doing. Algie wouldn't stand for that. Not his old mum.

Darnley   The kids was screaming . . .

Emmie   Oh, go on! They was all right. Bit of excitement for them. Anyway, they got to learn manners, ain't they? Arthur was well out of order.

Darnley   But you can't say but Algie ain't got a cruel streak, Mum. And he always goes straight for the jaguar.

Emmie   What was he meant to do? Just let it go? Just let his own mother be insulted? He's got to be free to express hisself, ain't he? Or are we living in Nazi cunting Germany all of a sudden? His grandfather fought and died for this country.

Darnley   What do you mean, died? He's in a home over in Ongar.

Emmie   Well, fought, anyway. You know what I mean. You don't have to pick me up on every little thing.

Darnley   He spent the whole war flogging nicked army vehicles. He had his own depot up by the North Circular there. With a big sign.

Emmie   He were building up a business. Something wrong with that now, is there?

Darnley   Sorry, Mum.

Emmie   Anyhow, Algie would never hurt his own kiss and king.

They all fall silent, gazing at each other as they consider this. They reach the same conclusion simultaneously and scatter, **Emmie** *and* **Chrissie** *pushing and shoving to get up the stairs first.*

Emmie   I'm going to get my bag.

Chrissie (*to* **Darnley**)   What shall I put in for you, Darn?

Darnley *is on his way towards the kitchen door.*

Darnley   I'll get the car out. Which car?

Emmie   The Merc.

Darnley   Have I got time to put a poultice on my parts?

Emmie   No!

Chrissie   I'll just put in some T-shirts and that.

They have all disappeared. **Darnley** *hurries back on and shouts up the stairs:*

Darnley   Don't forget my ointment!

He hurries off again and the stage is left empty and silent.

The silence is broken by the door chime playing 'In an English Country Garden'.

Silence.

It chimes again.

Nothing.

*We hear the faint sound of the front door being opened and closed and then a woman comes into the archway. This is **Allegra Tennyson**. Seeing that the room is empty, she comes in. **Allegra** is a winsome woman of thirty-five, dressed in a smart suit half a size too large.*

Allegra   Hello?

*She looks around the room. **Darnley** hurries back into the room and screeches to a halt when he sees her.*

Darnley   Who are you?

Allegra *turns and sees him.*

Allegra   Oh – you made me jump! You're Darnley, aren't you?

Darnley (*incredulously*)   Yes.

Allegra   I'm Allegra Tennyson.

*The name obviously means nothing to **Darnley**.*

Darnley   Oh. Right.

Allegra   Algie said I should meet him here.

Darnley   Algie did?

Allegra   He didn't want people waiting about outside the prison.

Darnley   No, I know.

He is at a loss.

Would you like a cup of Bovril?

Allegra   No, thanks. I'm a vegetarian.

Darnley   No, you just put hot water on it and –

Allegra   It's made from beef.

Darnley (*laughing*)   No! It's just this paste like. You can have it in sandwiches, and all.

Emmie, *now dressed and wearing a mink coat, clatters down the stairs, lugging a large, heavy suitcase.*

Emmie Darnley!

Darnley What?

Emmie You might give me a fucking hand!

Darnley There's someone here.

Emmie *stops dead. She cannot see* **Allegra** *yet.*

Emmie Not . . . ?

Darnley No – it's some woman.

Emmie Woman?

She gets to the bottom of the stairs and dumps the suitcase. She sees **Allegra**.

Emmie I know you.

Allegra Allegra Tennyson.

Emmie Allegra . . . ?

Allegra Tennyson. Distant cousin, I'm told.

Emmie Oh! Who is?

Allegra Alfred Tennyson.

Darnley What are we talking about here?

Allegra Alfred Tennyson.

Darnley Did he used to play for Millwall?

Allegra Oh, go on! Alfred Lord Tennyson? The poet?

Emmie He's not an idiot, you know. He's been on *Who Wants to Be a Millionaire*.

Allegra Oh, you lucky thing! I've always wanted to go on that. How did you get on?

Darnley Well . . .

Emmie   Never mind about that. What are you doing here, anyway?

Allegra   Algie said I should meet him here.

Emmie   Algie did? Why?

Allegra   Oh, I can't say. You'll have to ask him that. You don't remember me, do you?

Emmie   I seen you somewhere.

Allegra   Algie's trial? Mr Atkinson's junior.

Emmie   Oh, him! You know, Darnley – the barrister!

Darnley   Oh!

Emmie   Neither of you did him much fucking good, did you?

Allegra   No, I know. It was a difficult case to defend.

Emmie   He was innocent!

Allegra   He was all over the closed-circuit television! It looked as if he was auditioning for something.

Emmie   They got no right to use them things! It's an invasion of privacy. We've got rights, ain't we?

Allegra   No. Not if you're committing a crime.

Emmie   It's them that's committing the crime, mate. Spying on your every move – photographing you without so much as a by-your-leave – that's a crime, ain't it?

Allegra   No.

Emmie   Here! Whose fucking side are you on?

Darnley   But they don't like know you're going to commit a crime when they like instal them cameras, do they?

Allegra   Go on.

Darnley   And until you commit the crime, they're looking at you not committing a crime, right?

Allegra   This is good.

Darnley   So, so far as they know they're spying on innocent people. Which is wrong.

Allegra   You should have been a lawyer.

Darnley   Here! You hear that, Mum? She says I should of been a lawyer!

Emmie   You should of been a fucking human being, but it didn't work out right.

Chrissie   Darnley! Darnley!

Chrissie *has started down the stairs. She, too, is wearing a fur coat and is carrying two heavy bags.*

Chrissie   Where is the cunt?

Darnley   I'm here.

Chrissie   Well, give us a hand with these cunting bags, can't you, you idle sod.

Darnley   All right! All right!

He goes and meets her on the stairs and takes the bags.

There's someone here.

Chrissie   Who? Not . . . ?

Darnley   No – it's a lady lawyer woman.

Chrissie *sees* **Allegra**.

Chrissie   Oh.

Allegra   I'm here to meet Algie.

Darnley   Chrissie's my wife.

Allegra   How do you do?

Darnley   Listen – this'll make you laugh. She's also my –

Emmie   All right, Darnley!

Darnley   I thought she'd be interested. I mean, it's a legal conundrum, innit?

Allegra   Are you going away?

Chrissie   Going away?

Allegra   The bags.

Emmie   No! Just down the bottle bank. We're very hot on this global warning like.

Darnley   We're not going nowhere else.

Chrissie   No! Just down the – whatsit.

Emmie   Thought we'd have a bit of a clear-out, what with Algie coming home and everything.

Allegra   How lovely! Getting ready for the party?

Emmie   Party?

Allegra   You know – for Algie's release.

Darnley   We're not having no party.

Emmie   We're not the sort to make a fuss, you know.

Allegra   Oh.

Chrissie   We're like English.

Darnley   Easy come, easy go.

Chrissie   Never shall be slaves and that.

Darnley   Engerland! Engerland!

Allegra   Algie said you always had a party. He was looking forward to it. Me, too.

Darnley   Algie said?

Allegra   See all his old mates . . .

Chrissie   Oh, well – we're having just a little like get-together.

Emmie   Course we are!

Chrissie   Not a party, exactly.

Darnley   Just a few mates.

Emmie   Course we are!

Allegra   I brought a frock, in case. You can put me up, can't you?

Darnley   Up where?

Allegra   For the night. Just the one night. I know it's a bit of a liberty.

Emmie   Well . . .

Allegra   I'll get my bag from the car.

She heads for the hall.

Darnley   Bag?

Allegra   I'd like to hang the dress up. I don't want it all creased.

She goes. The others stare after her. We hear the front door close.

Emmie   What's her game, then?

Chrissie *goes to her bags and picks them up.*

Chrissie   Give us a hand with these.

Emmie   I'm not just leaving her in my house!

Chrissie   Why not?

Emmie   She's after the money.

Chrissie   There isn't any fucking money!

Emmie   She don't fucking know that, though, does she?

Chrissie   We haven't got time for this.

Emmie   Who is she? – That's what I'd like to know.

Darnley   We know who she is. She's that brief's assistant.

Emmie   So she says.

Darnley   You said you recognised her!

Emmie   I said I seen her before, I grant you . . .

Darnley   In the court!

Emmie   So she says. I never said that. That's why they wear them wigs, innit? – so's you won't recognise them in real life. Suppose she's really the filth?

Darnley   Nah!

Emmie   How does she know so much about Algie, then? You answer me that.

Darnley   We'd know her if she was local filth.

Chrissie *is staggering towards the hall with her two cases.*

Darnley   Or the Met.

Emmie   I did know her!

Darnley   Or the Thames Valley.

Emmie   She could be someone new, drafted in special.

Darnley   Or the West Midlands, I suppose, after the Birmingham Airport job.

Chrissie   Come on, you two!

Emmie   I'm not leaving her here. Suppose she is the filth? Algie's not going to thank us for leaving her here.

Chrissie   Algie's not going to thank us a lot, anyway.

Darnley   It could be the money. They want Algie to lead them to it!

Emmie   I'm not having her poking about in my things!

Darnley   There ain't nothing to poke.

Chrissie   We've got to get out of here!

Emmie   I'm calling Rocco.

Darnley (*startled*)   Rocco?

Emmie   Best get this sorted.

She takes her mobile phone out of her handbag.

Chrissie   Who is this Rocco?

Darnley   He's a hit man.

Chrissie   A hit man?

Darnley   You know – you give him money and he kills people for you.

Chrissie   We haven't got time for that! Come on!

Emmie   He's only over the road. We got to get it sorted, Chrissie.

Chrissie   Look, she ain't done nothing, we don't know who she is. Leave her.

Darnley   Tell you what, Mum. We'll tell her she can wait in her car. Not in the house because we're going down the thing.

Emmie   She'll still be waiting here when Algie gets back.

Darnley   We can't do nothing about that.

Chrissie   She's coming!

Emmie   I'm going to call Rocco.

Chrissie   No!

Allegra *comes in from the hall carrying a suitcase.*

Allegra   Here we are. I hope this isn't putting you out.

Darnley   We got to go down the thing – the global warning place.

Emmie *brushes him aside.*

Emmie   Here! We're not satisfied.

Allegra   Oh! What do you mean?

Emmie   About who you are and that.

Allegra   You know who I am. I'm –

Emmie   So you say.

Allegra   I've got my passport here.

Emmie   That don't prove nothing. I got four of them. What's your interest in our Algie?

Allegra   Oh . . . He'll tell you when he gets here.

Darnley   No. You'll tell us now.

Allegra   Look . . . All right. I'll tell you.

Darnley   That's more like it.

Allegra   Algie won't be pleased.

Emmie   Never mind about 'Algie won't be pleased'. I'll be the judge of that, if you don't mind. I'm his fucking mother.

Allegra   No, you're right. Okay. Well – you know how a man and a woman can sometimes look at one another and – oh, I don't know – just for a moment time seems to stand still?

Darnley   Mum was talking about that earlier. About when she was getting charvered by –

Emmie   Darnley!

Allegra   Anyway, the very first time I saw Algie – well, we saw each other – the very first time, we felt like that.

Emmie   Wait a minute, wait a minute!

Allegra   Suddenly nothing else existed for me except Algie. It was in a cell at Pentonville, but suddenly that didn't matter. Oh, I know it sounds soppy –

Emmie   Wait a minute. You said 'we'.

Allegra   What?

Emmie   You said 'we' felt like whatever it was you felt like.

Allegra   Well, we did.

Emmie   How do you know?

Allegra   Well, we've talked about it!

Chrissie   You been to see him?

Allegra   Of course I have!

Chrissie   He said as he didn't want no visitors!

Allegra   And we write every day.

Darnley   Write? You mean like letters?

Emmie   You write to him and he writes to you?

Allegra   He writes lovely letters.

Chrissie   What about?

Allegra   Well – you know. Look – Algie and I are getting married.

The other three stare at her, astounded. She looks from one to the other.

Is that so strange?

Chrissie   Married?

Darnley   Algie?

Allegra   What's wrong with that?

Chrissie   No, it's . . . We just never thought of Algie as . . .

Darnley   How did it come about, like?

Allegra   He bought me a ring.

She proffers her hand to show them. **Chrissie** *looks.*

Chrissie   Fucking hell!

Allegra   It's lovely, isn't it?

Darnley   Where did Algie like get the money?

Allegra   Oh, I used mine. He told me to choose it and he'd pay me back when he got out. It was instantaneous, you know how it is, sometimes. As soon as we saw each other. I was embarrassed at first – he just stared.

Darnley   No, he does that. He won't wear his glasses, see? He stares at people, trying to make out their like features. He's scared he'll go talking to a mop or something.

Allegra   I don't think it was that.

Darnley   It's served him well, mind. It frightens the shit out of people, having him stare at them like that. 'Algie's ray', they call it. Like death-ray, like. Cougher Norris broke down and confessed as how he'd grassed Algie up once when Algie kept looking at him. Algie told me after, he was only trying to work out who Cougher was. Mind you, he had very like undistinguishable features, did Cougher. He was on hundreds of police line-ups – nobody ever picked him out, though nine times out of ten it was him they was after. Poor old Cougher. Even when they found his body, they couldn't identify him. Not until they brought his mum in and she said, 'I think it's Basil.' That's what she used to call Cougher.

Emmie *has remained frozen until now, staring at* **Allegra**.

Emmie   Algie never said nothing to me.

Allegra   He wanted to keep it as a surprise.

Emmie   Oh, he did. He did. I just got to make a call.

She goes towards the kitchen, taking her mobile from her pocket as she goes.

Darnley   Who you calling, Mum?

Emmie (*annoyed*)   The bottle bank. Let them know we'll be late.

She exits.

Allegra   If someone could just show me my room . . . ?

Chrissie   Oh – yes. Up the stairs, third door on your right.

Allegra   Thanks.

She goes up the stairs with her suitcase.

This is all right, is it?

Chrissie   Oh, yes. Third door on the right. Take your time.

Allegra *goes.*

Darnley (*to* **Chrissie**)   You all right?

Chrissie   What do you mean?

Darnley   You seem a bit – you know.

Emmie *comes back into the room.*

Emmie   Fucking engaged.

Chrissie   Well, try again!

Darnley   Look – let's just get out of here.

Chrissie   No! We're not leaving her here!

Darnley   You've changed your tune, ain't you?

Chrissie (*to* **Emmie**)   Try again!

Emmie *dials again.*

Chrissie   Cow! Coming here with her lies!

Darnley   What lies?

Emmie   Still engaged. They always give themselves away, don't they?

Darnley   How do you mean?

Emmie   She's been writing letters to Algie, yes?

Darnley   Yes.

Emmie   Algie's been writing back, yes?

Darnley   So?

Emmie   Since when has Algie been doing reading and writing, may I ask?

Darnley   Oh! Oh – I see what you mean. Hey!

Emmie   What did I say as soon as I clapped eyes on her? Well dodgy, that's what I said.

Chrissie   You think Algie would go and get married out of the blue like that? Marriage is a honourable estate, for fuck's sake!

Darnley   He might of took lessons inside. For the writing, like.

Chrissie   And marry a woman like that? All that posh talk!

Emmie   We may be like just ordinary people, but at least we've got no cunting side! They're like a rag to a bull to me, that type.

Chrissie   What about her clothes, then? Excuse me, sorry, have I missed something? Is it suddenly 1983 all of a sudden? Algie wouldn't waste his breath looking at a woman like that!

Emmie   And her shoes!

Chrissie   She's filth. Definite filth. Soon as Algie gets back she'll have us all banged up. Try Rocco again. Go on.

Emmie *dials again.*

Darnley (*to* **Chrissie**)   I don't know what's the matter with you.

Chrissie   You keep out of this!

Darnley   First of all you're –

Chrissie   Oh, for Christ's sake shut up, Darnley!

Allegra *has appeared again on the stairs.* **Emmie** *hangs up hurriedly.*

Allegra   Is it all right if I use the bathroom?

Emmie   Bathroom? Fine, darling, fine! Use whatever you like.

Allegra   Thanks.

She starts to go up the stairs again, then turns back.

Oh, by the way . . .

Chrissie   What?

Allegra   I've got to get down to the safety deposit place before it closes.

They all stare at her, unable to speak.

Get Algie's money, so we can be off first thing tomorrow.

Emmie   Money?

Allegra   Yes. Could you let me have the key?

Emmie   Key?

Allegra   Algie gave you the key, he said.

Emmie   Oh, the key! Oh, I don't know where that is, darling.

Allegra *frowns. She comes slowly down the stairs.*

Allegra   Oh?

Emmie   Oh – where did I put it now? Well, it wouldn't do you much good without the password, anyway.

Allegra   Algie told me the password.

Emmie   Oh. Well, I'm sorry, dear, I can't think where I put that blessed key.

Allegra (*menacingly*)   You'd better think really hard, Mrs Packer.

Emmie   Well, I am thinking, darling. You know how it is – you put something in a special place –

Allegra   Really hard and really fast.

Darnley   Now then, now then . . .

Allegra   Stay out of this, cunt-face. (*To* **Emmie**.) The next time I come down those fucking stairs, I want that fucking key.

Emmie (*doubtfully*)   Well, I'll –

Allegra   Otherwise I might think there's something dodgy going on.

She starts up the stairs again.

Emmie   Dodgy? No!

Allegra *has gone.*

Emmie   Nice language, I must say!

Chrissie   She's got no respect.

Emmie   What did I tell you? Right! That does it.

She starts to dial on her mobile again.

Chrissie   The cow!

Emmie   What did I tell you?

Chrissie (*to* **Darnley**)   Here! Give me a key!

Darnley   What key?

Chrissie   Any key! Don't matter.

Darnley *takes a key ring from his pocket and starts to remove one of the keys.*

Chrissie   She won't know the difference, will she? And by the time she finds out . . .

Emmie *speaks into the phone.*

Emmie   Rocco? This is Emmie Packer from over the road. How are you, love? No, fine. Yes. Rocco – we got this little job for you, darling. Here. Yes. Yes. Well, right here.

Chrissie   Now!

Emmie   Yes – right now. Can you come over? See you in a minute, then.

She switches off the phone and puts it back in her pocket.

He's coming over. Right. As soon as he gets here, we get her into the kitchen. He can do it in there. I'm not having this carpet ruined. Then Darnley can dispose of the body.

Chrissie   Leave it here! Who cares?

Emmie   No! Show a bit of respect. It can go under the patio.

Chrissie   We haven't got time for that!

Darnley   There's no more room under there, anyway.

Emmie   All right, then, you'll have to drive her to the gravel pit. That water's thirty foot deep.

Chrissie   Algie's on his way!

Emmie   And he's not going to want dead bodies all over the house, is he? Not on his first day home.

Chrissie   That's his fucking problem!

Emmie   We do it properly or we don't do it at all. You just don't understand the old-fashioned values, do you?

Chrissie   Well, he'll have to be fucking quick, that's all I can say!

Darnley   Oh, Rocco'll be quick, don't you fret.

Chrissie   Who is he, anyway?

Emmie   He's a professional hit man. Top of his trade.

Chrissie   No, I know, but he's like Italian, is he?

Darnley   No, no, no. He just calls hisself Rocco.

Emmie   Rocco Dimaggio. That's from – oh – years back. He was very keen to join the Mafia in them days. Looked on it as a sort of gold star, like being a mason. He used to read all them books about the Mafia, see all the films. 'You know where you are with Casa Nostra,' he used to say. Anyhow, he met this bloke in a pub in Chigwell, said he could get him in. Rocco filled in the forms and everything and give this bloke a thousand quid and never saw him again. He was ever so cut up about it. Especially after changing his name and everything.

Darnley   Eric Magee, his real name was.

Allegra   Whose real name?

The **Packers** *are startled by the appearance of* **Allegra** *on the stairs.*

Emmie   Oh, just this friend of ours.

Darnley   He might be coming over in a minute. Just to see us, like. Just a social call.

Chrissie   Give Algeria the key, Darnley.

Darnley   Oh – right.

He hands a key to **Allegra**, *who puts it in her pocket without looking at it.*

Allegra   Good. Thank you.

Darnley   It was in the . . .

Emmie   Where we keep the keys, like.

Allegra   Good. This is such a beautiful house, Mrs Packer.

Emmie   What do you mean?

Allegra   You can see for miles from my window. Is that Dagenham over in – oh – that direction?

Emmie   I don't know, I never looked. You're interested in geography, are you?

Allegra   I like to know where I am.

Emmie   Ah!

The doorbell rings.

Darnley   That'll be Rocco.

He goes towards the front door.

Allegra   Is that your friend?

Emmie   I hope so. You wouldn't want him as a enemy.

Darnley *comes back with* **Rocco**. **Rocco** *is seventy-five and slow-moving. He is a cheerful, jokey character, usually smiling, dressed in baseball jacket and cap, and carpet slippers.*

Darnley   Here he is!

Rocco *strikes an attitude.*

Rocco   Ta-da! The Italian Stallion!

Emmie   How are you, Rocco?

Rocco   Oh, mustn't grumble, you know.

Emmie   Why not? Have a grumble – enjoy yourself!

Rocco   My leg's giving me gyp, mind. I can't bear to put it on the floor, some mornings. The doctor says it's smoking.

Emmie   I can't see no smoke.

She laughs.

Rocco   Always got a joke, ain't you, Em?

Emmie   Doctors don't know nothing. What do doctors know? How is smoking a few cigarettes going to affect your leg? Answer me that.

Darnley   Here! You'll never guess what happened to me yesterday.

Emmie (*to* **Rocco**)   Oh, you haven't met Algeria, have you?

Allegra   How do you do? It's Allegra, actually.

Rocco   Pleased to meet you, whatever your name is.

Allegra   Algeria's a country.

Darnley   A what? Sorry, Mum.

Emmie   Would you like a cup of tea, Rocco?

Rocco   No, I just had my breakfast.

Emmie   Coffee, then?

Rocco   No, not really.

Emmie   Oh, go on! Tell you what, Allegra, could you make Rocco a nice cup of coffee?

Allegra (*looking at her watch*)   Well, I've got to get down to the . . .

Emmie   Oh, they don't close till five. I believe. Might as well get used to the place. Now you're one of the family, almost.

Allegra   Yes, of course.

Emmie   We've only got the instant, is that all right, Rocco?

Rocco   I like expresso, really.

Emmie (*patiently*)   But Nescafé Gold will do just this once.

Rocco   All right.

Allegra   Anybody else like one?

Darnley   Go on then. I'll have a nice cup of Bovril.

Chrissie   Darnley!

Darnley   What?

Emmie   You don't need Bovril, Darnley.

Darnley   Yes, I do. In my big mug. You can't miss it – it's got a 'D' on it. That's for Darnley. We all used to have them, but mine's the only one hasn't got broke. There was one with 'E' on it – that was Mum's. There was one with –

Emmie   That's one coffee, one Bovril, Allegra.

Allegra   Fine. Won't be a minute.

She goes into the kitchen. **Emmie** *turns on* **Darnley**, *furious.*

Emmie   What's the matter with you, you great nana!

Darnley   What?

Emmie (*mimicking him*) There's one with 'C' on it – for cunt. One with –

Chrissie What does he want Bovril for, anyway?

Darnley I like it! Anyway, I'm in real pain here! I got to like replace my juices. (*To* **Rocco**.) What happened was –

Emmie (*to* **Rocco**) She's it.

Rocco What – her in the kitchen?

Emmie All right?

Rocco Fine.

He shows no sign of moving.

Chrissie We're in a bit of a hurry here, Mr Dimaggio.

Rocco Oh, right. I thought I was having my coffee first.

Emmie No, that was just to get her into the kitchen.

Rocco Oh, I see! A ruse!

Chrissie We're in a real hurry. I'm sorry.

Rocco No, no. Fine. You really got this thought out. You mean, do it in there, like?

Emmie That's it.

Rocco *starts towards the kitchen, then turns back.*

Rocco I done some of my best work in kitchens. You know what I hate?

Darnley What?

Rocco Living rooms. One shot goes astray and there's expensive ornaments to consider. In a kitchen, you see, it's only going to be your Pyrex jug or similar. Better still, a frying pan. It'll be my usual terms, of course.

Darnley Terms?

Emmie Oh, yes, of course.

She fumbles in her handbag.

We've only got a fifty-pound note, I'm afraid.

Rocco *looks from one to the other of them.*

Rocco   I ain't got no change.

Emmie *crosses to him and tucks the note into his pocket.*

Rocco   Whoo! Thanks, Emmie. Here we go, then. Off to the races.

He goes to the kitchen door, takes a deep breath and goes in.

Emmie, **Darnley** *and* **Chrissie** *stand watching the door. Silence.*

Chrissie   He's taking his time.

Emmie   He's a craftsman. One of the old school.

They continue to watch. Silence.

Chrissie   Here – this global warning, what's that all about?

Emmie   Oh, it's when the Russians are coming, innit? In their like rockets. You get four minutes warning.

Chrissie   So what's the bottles for?

Emmie   How should I know? Throw at the Russians, I suppose.

Darnley   No – they melt them down and make Spitfires. Well . . . weaponry. Radioactive particles, like.

Silence.

Perhaps he's strangling her.

Emmie   No, no, no. Always uses a Biretta, famous for it.

Chrissie   Come on, come on!

Silence again. Then the kitchen door opens and **Rocco** *comes out, carrying a tray with two mugs on it.*

Rocco (*to* **Darnley**)   There you go, Darn. One Bovril. Get that down you, son.

Darnley *takes a mug from the tray.*

Rocco   I forgot my shooter.

Emmie   Oh, shit!

Rocco   Left it on the hall table. I'll go over and get it.

He starts towards the front door.

Emmie   Stay there! You can use Algie's.

Rocco   Oh, I don't know . . .

Emmie   Stay!

She is already heading for the stairs.

Rocco (*anxiously*)   I can't return a fee, you know. We don't have the procedures for it.

Emmie   I'll procedure you, mate, if you fuck this up.

She goes off up the stairs. **Rocco** *explains to* **Darnley** *and* **Chrissie**.

Rocco   We just can't do it. All the book work makes it uneconomic.

Darnley   Good Bovril, Rocco.

Chrissie *slumps on to the sofa.*

Chrissie   We're all going to die.

Darnley   How many spoons you put in?

Rocco   Two.

Darnley   Ah.

Rocco   And just a little pinch of white pepper.

Darnley   No!

Rocco   Picked that up down Upton Park.

Darnley   Really?

Chrissie It's twenty past eleven. In an hour I'll be lying – a lifeless chunk, my lifeblood oozing away.

Rocco Course, this would never have happened if Doreen had been here.

Darnley How come?

Rocco She used to check me before I left the house. See I had everything. I was always forgetting to put my teeth in.

Darnley Bit of a tragedy, her going like that, wasn't it?

Rocco I'll never forgive myself.

Darnley No, I don't think you should blame yourself, Rocco.

Rocco If I close my eyes, I can see her now, as she was in her last moments.

Darnley Go on!

Rocco No – straight up. Standing there, dressed all in white, an apple on her head, re-enacting the legend of Robin Hood.

Darnley For the kids, wasn't it?

Rocco The grandchildren.

Darnley They must of been upset.

Rocco I don't see them no more. Little Reg – well, he grew up to be the Romford Strangler, of course.

Darnley Oh, right.

Rocco Topped hisself as the rozzers moved in for the arrest. And Imogen – well, she's been in and out of that institute all her life. She's a bit funny in the head, like. I don't see her.

Allegra *comes in from the kitchen.*

Allegra What a lovely kitchen!

Chrissie   Oh, Christ!

Allegra   No, you should see mine. Well, you shouldn't, actually – I'd be ashamed. Yours looks so new and everything!

Emmie *hurries down the stairs, revolver in hand. She stops and puts the gun in her pocket as she hears* **Allegra***'s voice.*

Allegra   You and Darnley live here with Emmie, do you?

Darnley   At the moment we do, yes. Just temporary, like.

Allegra   Algie, too?

Darnley   We're a close family.

Emmie   Oh, that coffee don't half smell good!

Darnley   No, mine's Bovril, Mum.

Emmie   I wouldn't mind a cup, myself.

Allegra   Shall I make you one, Mrs Packer?

Emmie   Oh, would you, dear? Not too much trouble?

Allegra   Course not.

She goes towards the kitchen.

Darnley   Have we got time for this, Mum?

Emmie *loses control for a moment.*

Emmie   Jesus Christ!

She regains control.

Course we have, Darnley.

Allegra   Won't be a sec.

She goes into the kitchen. **Emmie** *hurries across to* **Rocco** *and hands him the gun.*

Emmie   There you are. It's loaded. I've always kept something from every one of Algie's jobs.

Rocco   Sort of memento, like.

Emmie   That's it.

Rocco   You're a good mum, Emmie. I've always said. Mind you, I prefer my Biretta. It's the Italian connection, I suppose. It always –

Emmie   Get on with it.

Rocco   Oh. Right.

He goes towards the kitchen. Once again, **Emmie**, **Darnley** *and* **Chrissie** *wait. This time, their expectations are satisfied. There is the loud report of a gun, followed by the crash and clatter of a rack of saucepans being knocked over on to a tiled floor. This is followed by another shot, the whine of a bullet ricocheting and* **Rocco**'s *anguished voice.*

Rocco (*offstage*)   Ow!

Emmie *and* **Chrissie** *look at each other, puzzled.*

Rocco   Oh, Gawd! Oh!

Chrissie   What's the matter with him?

Emmie   Darnley.

Darnley   What?

Emmie *jerks her head in the direction of the kitchen.*

Darnley   There's bullets flying around in there!

Emmie   See what's the matter with him.

Unwillingly, and with considerable trepidation, **Darnley** *goes into the kitchen.*

Chrissie   You know what he's gone and done, don't you?

Darnley *appears in the doorway again.*

Darnley   He's gone and shot hisself.

Chrissie   I told you!

Emmie   What about the girl?

Darnley   She's dead.

Emmie   Get Rocco out of there.

Darnley   Give us a hand, Chrissie.

Chrissie   Oh, Jesus!

*She follows **Darnley** into the kitchen. **Emmie** holds the door open and watches.*

Emmie   He's not bleeding, is he?

Darnley (*offstage*)   Course he's bleeding!

Emmie   Well, put something under him, then! You know what blood's like. One of them plastic bags. That's it. Well, roll him over on to it. That's it.

*She stands back to allow **Darnley** and **Chrissie** through the door. They are carrying the semi-conscious **Rocco** between them with a black rubbish bag under him.*

Rocco   I'm a goner, Emmie!

Emmie   No you're not.

Darnley *and* **Chrissie** *have taken **Rocco** to the sofa and are about to put him on it.*

Emmie   Keep that bag under him.

Rocco   It's that tile floor done for me. Oh! Oh, Christ!

They prop him up on the sofa.

Emmie   Get another bag for under his feet. In case it seeps down his trousers.

Darnley *hurries back into the kitchen.*

Rocco   Bleeding tile floors!

Emmie   Get his jacket off.

*She and **Chrissie** start to take off **Rocco**'s jacket.*

Rocco   Oh! Oh! Oh, it hurts, Emmie!

Emmie   Well, it would do, wouldn't it? You gone and fucking shot yourself, you stupid get.

Rocco   Bullets don't half bounce about off them fashionable quarry tiles.

They have got his jacket off. His shirt is soaked with blood on one side at about waist level. **Emmie** *undoes the shirt and looks at the wound.*

Emmie   It's just a flesh wound, Rocco.

Rocco   No, it ain't. I can feel it nuzzling there in my tripes.

Emmie   You're all right. Chrissie – go and get a couple of clean tea-towels and some hot water.

Chrissie *goes, bumping into* **Darnley** *as he comes out of the kitchen with a plastic bag.*

Emmie   Get this cleaned up, you'll be right as rain. (*To* **Darnley**.) Just put it under his feet.

Darnley *kneels down and arranges the bag under* **Rocco**'s *feet.*

Emmie   Now get the other one down the gravel pit.

Darnley   He looks bad.

Emmie   Never mind about that.

Darnley   Is it still in there – the bullet?

Emmie   How should I know? He says it is.

Darnley   Well, have a look. See if there's an exit wound.

Emmie   How do I do that?

Darnley   Just look! The hole will be bigger than the one where it went in.

Emmie   I can't see nothing. Why bigger?

Darnley   Well, it's that shape like of the bullet, innit? I mean the front bit's got the point, but the back bit's like bigger because it hasn't. So . . .

Emmie (*losing patience*)   Well, I can't see nothing. It's all blood. He says it's still in there.

Rocco   It is. I can feel it.

Emmie   Oh, you're back with us, are you?

Rocco   A sort of nudging, heavy feeling.

Darnley   Well, it's lead, you see.

Emmie   Good for you – bit of iron.

Darnley   No, Mum, it's lead.

Emmie   Well – it's all metal, innit?

Darnley   He'll get lead poisoning or something.

Emmie   Well, I can't help that. What am I meant to do, put the tongs up his jacksie?

Rocco (*terrified*)   Here!

Darnley   He ought to be in the hospital. We can't just leave him.

Emmie   He'll be all right.

Rocco   I'll be all right, son. Oh, I didn't know it hurt like this.

Darnley   Being shot? Bound to hurt a bit, innit?

Chrissie *comes back from the kitchen, carrying a bowl of water and some tea-towels.*

Chrissie   How is he?

Emmie   He's all right.

Darnley   It hurts, he says.

Emmie   Give us one of them tea-towels, Chrissie love.

Chrissie *does so.*

Darnley   I said, 'It's bound to hurt a bit, innit?'

Emmie   Will you get off down the gravel pit!

Darnley   All right, all right!

He goes off through the kitchen door. **Emmie** *is tending* **Rocco**.

Emmie   Rocco! Don't you go to sleep.

Chrissie   Here! There's her bag upstairs!

Emmie   Bag?

Chrissie   That Algeria's. We don't want to leave that here for Algie to find. If he thinks we've had the filth here . . . !

She goes towards the stairs.

Emmie   We won't be here, anyway.

Chrissie   I'm not chancing he won't catch up with us.

She goes off up the stairs.

Emmie   You all right, Rocco?

Rocco *groans.*

Emmie   You're all right.

Rocco   I was the executioner, see? Unswerving. Emotionless. You get found guilty by your peers, I'm there to carry out the verdict. Mr Cool. Firm but fair.

Emmie   Only if they paid you.

Rocco   I'm not a fucking charity, am I? But I never thought about it hurting. Never considered it, even. I was above all that. Ow!

Emmie   Hold still, will you?

Rocco   What are you doing? Blimey, just leave me, will you?

Emmie   I can't just leave you. You're bleeding all over everything.

Chrissie *starts slowly down the stairs. She is reading from a single sheet of paper. She stops halfway down and looks down at* **Emmie**.

Chrissie   Here, Emmie.

Emmie (*to* **Rocco**)   I'll get some safety pins and fix a sort of pad.

Chrissie   Emmie.

Emmie   What?

Chrissie   I found a letter in her bag.

Emmie   Don't bother with that. Get me another couple of tea-towels.

Chrissie   It's from Algie.

Emmie   Get away! Why would she have a letter from Algie?

Chrissie   It's to her.

Emmie   But he can't –

Chrissie   He can now.

Emmie *straightens up and crosses to meet* **Chrissie** *at the bottom of the stairs.*

Emmie   What's it say?

Chrissie (*reading*)   'Dearest Algeria, In one week I will be free. I will meet you at my mum's house like what we said. Then – '

Emmie   Let me see! Let me see!

She peers over **Chrissie**'s *shoulder.*

Emmie   Oh, look! 'mum'! Look at the writing! He's written 'mum'.

Chrissie   All right! All right!

Emmie   He could never do that before. Ah – look! It's all like almost joined-up writing, and all! I knew he could do it!

She wipes away a tear. **Chrissie** *shrugs her off.*

Chrissie   'I will meet you at my mum's house, like what we said. Then we will go to Rio. We will get married. I love you, Algeria. Algie.' Oh, Gawd.

Emmie   What's Rio?

Chrissie   Rio de Janerio, I suppose. You know what we've gone and done, don't you?

Emmie   What?

Chrissie   We've spent all his like money. Now we've gone and had his fiancée killed and all.

Curtain.

Act Two

One year later. A first-floor flat with whitewashed walls, an ornate wrought-iron grille outside the window and a slow-moving fan on the ceiling. Brilliant sunshine illuminates the bullfight posters on the wall. The furniture is cheap and well-worn.

The stage is empty and the only sound that of muffled Latin American music coming from downstairs.

After a moment there is the rattle of a key in the lock and **Darnley** *comes in. He is wearing tight-fitting black satin bell-bottoms and a shirt with big ruffled sleeves, such as used to be worn by members of a rhumba band. He calls.*

Darnley   Chrissie?

No reply. He shakes his head, irritated. He throws the pair of maracas he is carrying on to the sofa and goes to one of the two bedroom doors. He opens it and looks in.

Chrissie? Oh, sorry. Get out of there, will you?

He shuts the door again. Disconsolate, he picks up the maracas and accompanies himself with them as he tries out a few dance steps.

The bedroom door **Darnley** *opened opens again, and* **Rocco** *heaves slowly into view, supporting himself on a Zimmer frame. He is wearing pyjama bottoms and a vest.*

Darnley   You're not meant to sleep in there.

Rocco   I got to sleep somewhere!

Darnley   The sofa, that's where you sleep.

Rocco   How am I meant to sleep on that thing?

Darnley   That room's for Chrissie and me. Ain't you never going to get dressed?

Rocco   It's too hot to wear clothes.

Darnley   You seen Chrissie?

Rocco   Not since first thing. What's the point getting dressed, anyhow? I can't go nowhere, can I? I couldn't manage the stairs. Right mess that so-called doctor of yours made of me.

Darnley   Oh, leave it out, Rocco.

Rocco   He wasn't no doctor!

Darnley   Course he was. You'd of been dead now if it hadn't been for him.

Rocco   He was a bleeding vet.

Darnley   Course he weren't. He were an old friend of my dad's.

Rocco   I saw the sign as you drove in! What's a doctor doing living at a race track?

Darnley   How should I know? Perhaps he likes a flutter.

Rocco   And why did he keep talking about my fetlocks, then? And the bullet going in my flank?

Darnley   Anyway, you're all right now.

Rocco   Oh, yes. Oh, yes. If you call this 'all right'. That anaesthetic he give me, I didn't come round for three days!

Darnley   Oh, bollocks!

Rocco   The syringe was big as a milk bottle! I been numb all the way down my left leg ever since.

Darnley   Look – shut up for a minute, will you? I've got to rehearse.

Rocco   Rehearse! Prancing about like some Peruvian poof!

Darnley   It pays the rent, mate, don't you fret.

He starts to dance again, then stops.

Here! I had this weird dream last night. Woke up in a terrible sweat. What I dreamed was, I dreamed about Algeria – you remember, that bint you offed. Only somehow it weren't Algeria, it were Chrissie – you know how dreams are. And she was coming towards me and her eyes was all swirling and funny and I held out my arms to her, like, and I suddenly realised she had this bloody great knife in her hand. And she kept saying, 'A nice little slice, Darnley. A nice little slice.'

Rocco   Go on.

Darnley   No, then I woke up. What's that all about, do you reckon?

Rocco   How the fuck should I know?

Darnley   I don't know, I just thought – a man of your years, you might have learned something about the mysteries of the human heart. Wisdom and that.

Rocco   Nah!

Darnley   Oh.

Rocco   It don't work like that, son. And it's not as if I ain't opened myself up to the possibility of learning.

Darnley   No?

Rocco   Oh, no. After Doreen died, I stood by her graveside and I looked up to Heaven and I said, 'Tell me, Lord, tell me! What the fuck's it all about?' Nothing.

Darnley   Nothing at all?

Rocco   Not a fucking word. No clap of thunder. Nothing.

Darnley   I don't remember the funeral.

Rocco   Oh, it was very quiet. Just family. Very nice, though. Couple of prayers we got out the newspaper, then we had to get the patio back in place before it got light.

Darnley   Here's Chrissie now!

This as he hears a key in the lock. The door opens and **Emmie** *comes in.*

Darnley (*disappointed*)   Oh.

Emmie   And hasta la fucking vista to you, mate! What do you mean, 'oh'?

Darnley I thought you was Chrissie.

Emmie She not back yet?

Darnley No. Eduardo's getting really pissed off with Chrissie.

Emmie *is wearing a long smock which she unbuttons as she goes to the kitchen table by the window.*

Emmie She's got to get her fucking nails done, ain't she?

Darnley Doesn't take all day.

Emmie Look nice for his customers.

Darnley It's the second day this week she just hasn't turned up.

Rocco What you got for supper, Emmie?

Emmie Here.

She has a variety of packages hooked to a belt under her smock. She starts to unhook them and put them on the table.

Nice chicken.

Rocco Looks like an old boiler to me.

Emmie Get off! Tender as a woman's heart, that is.

Rocco In that case, I'll have the beef.

Emmie Oh, he will have his little joke! Nice roast potatoes. Some sort of veg, don't ask me what. They have funny veg here. And four caramel things for afters.

Rocco You get all this on the staff discount, do you?

Emmie *winks at* **Darnley**.

Emmie Something like that.

Rocco They're very good, ain't they?

Emmie Oh, fucking wonderful, they are! You sit at one of their fucking tills for ten hours a day for about two quid an hour, they let you have a penny off a packet of wine gums.

Darnley   She wasn't going nowhere else, was she?

Emmie   Who?

Darnley   Chrissie! Like after she'd had her nails done.

Emmie   How the fuck should I know! You're the one who's meant to be married to her.

Darnley   She's never settled here.

Emmie   None of us have ever settled here. I mean, what a dump! Have you seen them? The people?

Rocco   I haven't seen nobody!

He sits on the sofa and tries to make himself comfortable.

Emmie   I mean, I know it's not their fault, but they're not like us, are they? Little piggy eyes – all this hair. I mean, you see a family of them coming down the street and you know just from looking at them that they can't wait to get home and start interfering with each other.

Darnley   They do have big families.

Rocco   The last person I spoke to, apart from you lot, was a year ago, back home, that morning, the postman. He rang my bell with a parcel – my latest delivery from the Franklyn Mint. 'Famous Shoes from History in Hand-Painted Bone China'. Twenty-four of them, there were going to be.

Darnley   How big were they?

Rocco *holds up his thumb and forefinger to indicate an inch.*

Rocco   About like that. Exquisite workmanship. You could see every lace-hole. I'd only had two – Queen Elizabeth's one she had when she stepped in the mud, and Julius Caesar's sandal when he did something. Number three was the one George Washington wore for cutting down the apple tree. I was saving it to open after my dinner. Then you phoned.

Emmie   We're having a serious discussion here, Rocco.

Rocco   No – I'm just saying. They'll be piling up. Twenty-nine-ninety a pop, and I'm not getting the benefit.

Emmie   What the fuck benefit are you going to get from a lot of china shoes?

Rocco   They're informative, hand-crafted, and objects of beauty in their own right!

Emmie   Objects of bollocks. What was I saying?

She starts to pick up the food from the table to take it into the kitchen.

Darnley   About the people.

Emmie   No, but the stuff they eat! I mean, I see it day after day at work. It nearly makes me heave sometimes. Bits of animals a doctor wouldn't recognise! It can't be good for them. I mean, there should be laws, shouldn't there? Chops, yes; steaks, all right; legs, fine; but glands you draw the line at.

Darnley   Live and let live, that's what I say.

Emmie   Yeah, but that's because you're a cunt.

She goes into the kitchen.

Darnley   I don't know what's got into her today.

Rocco   You know what day it is?

Darnley   I dunno. Tuesday?

Rocco   One year today since we arrived here. Exactly.

Darnley (*uninterested*)   Oh.

Rocco   We're not getting any younger, you know. Well, I'm not, I don't know about you.

Darnley   What are you going on about?

Rocco *looks apprehensively towards the kitchen.*

Rocco   I was on the dog today.

Darnley   Who to?

Rocco   Never mind who to.

Darnley   Oh, blimey.

Rocco   No listen. This person I was speaking to –

Darnley   What person?

Rocco   What I'm saying is – why don't you and me – you know.

He repeatedly jerks his head in the direction of the main door.

Darnley *looks at him blankly.*

Rocco   Do a runner.

Darnley   Runner?

Rocco   You and me, like.

Darnley   Where to?

Rocco   Back home.

Darnley   Have you gone raving mad?

Rocco   No – listen.

Darnley   Algie would be all over us before our feet touched the ground, even.

Rocco   Maybe he would. Maybe he wouldn't.

Darnley   Why wouldn't he?

Rocco   Because he wouldn't. Maybe.

Darnley *stares at* **Rocco**.

Darnley   You never called Algie!

Rocco   Listen –

Darnley   You did! You called Algie!

Rocco   Shhh! He can't trace the call. I done it on Emmie's mobile.

Darnley   You berk!

Rocco   No – listen.

Darnley   What you want to call Algie for, for fuck's sake?

Rocco   Don't worry! I was – what-do-you-call-it? – discreet.
I know Algie of old.

Darnley   I didn't know you knew him at all. Not really
knew him.

Rocco (*evasively*)   No – well . . .

Darnley   What do you mean, you know him of old?

Rocco   Well – we did a bit of business together – oh, ages ago.

Darnley   What business?

Rocco   Well – you know – my usual line.

Darnley   He put out a contract on someone?

Rocco   Yes – well – something like that.

Darnley   Who?

Rocco   Oh, I can't tell you that, son. Professional ethics.

Darnley   Get out of here, you useless old tit!

Rocco   No, that's what people always say. But we have a
code, you know. Let me just say this – someone got this young
bint in trouble.

Darnley   Yes . . . ?

Rocco   Well, there you are. And your brother's sense of
honour and decency was offended.

Darnley   What young bint?

Rocco   That I cannot tell you.

Darnley   But you killed her.

Rocco   No, no, no, no, no.

Darnley   Well, who did you kill?

Rocco   The bloke that put her up the duff.

Darnley   Where does Algie come into this?

Rocco   Well, he took out the contract, like.

Darnley   Why?

Rocco   Well, you know how fond he is of your mum.

Darnley   My mum?

Rocco   He didn't want her hurt. Her, like, feelings. And – well – it concerned a member of her family.

Darnley   Who?

Rocco   Well, the bint that got into trouble was your cousin Vera.

Darnley   Vera? The one with the limp?

Rocco   That's her. The ironwork round the leg.

Darnley (*laughing*)   Who'd put her up the stick? I mean, I don't wish her no harm but . . . If there was a competition for Miss Ugly . . . He must of been desperate, whoever he was. She'd suck you in and blow you out in green froth.

Rocco   No, no. Vera had her charms. She had these like enormous knockers.

Darnley   Granted, but –

Rocco   To your dad that was a prime attraction.

Darnley   My dad?

Rocco   Oh, shit.

Darnley   My dad?

Rocco   Forget I said that. I was just using him as a like sample. I mean, when he was young he was always hanging round that corset shop in the Roman Road.

Darnley   Don't give me that!

Rocco   It's true! I mean, we all appreciate such things, I'm sure, but he was obsessive. Take your mum – all respect to her and that – she was always a lady – but when she was younger she had these most gigantic hooters. They was the talk of Barking, among the discriminating. Wapping, too, I believe. They used to have meetings about them. Informal, I grant you, but there was many an eye moist with remembrance when they erected the Dome.

Darnley   What's this got to do with my dad?

Realisation dawns.

You never killed my fucking father!

Rocco   Only by way of business, son. And I'll say this for young Algie – he paid up like a good 'un.

Darnley   We always thought it was Olly Oliver's gang – the way his body was dumped on our doorstep and everything.

Rocco   That was my idea. That was where I was clever.

Darnley   And Algie put on like he was distracted with grief. Went round for months vowing vengeance.

Rocco   No, he was upset. It can't have been easy for him, can it? It was a like moral dilemma.

Darnley   Whether to have his dad murdered?

Rocco   That's it. That or have his mother heartbroken. When he come to me he was a good five or six minutes wrestling with his conscience. It was a pitiful sight. He said to me, 'Rocco,' he said, 'I'm on the corns of a dilemma.' But eventually he said, 'Oh, fuck it.'

Darnley   So, that young Teddy Drew is my dad's son?

Rocco   That's it. Doing his first stretch now.

Darnley   My half-brother.

Rocco   I suppose he is. He's a fine lad.

Darnley   Fucking hell! I'm collecting relatives like confetti. They just keep raining down. You and me aren't related, are we?

Rocco   I don't think so, son.

Darnley   That's something, I suppose. Only, I seem to be related to most of Essex.

Rocco   Anyway – as I say, I spoke to him this a.m.

Darnley   Who? Oh – Algie. I just can't get my head round this.

Rocco   I mean, I'm going round the twist here, Darnley.

Darnley   We're all going round the twist.

Rocco   So I thought, if I have a word with Algie . . .

Darnley   If you've let on to Algie where we are . . . !

Rocco   I told you! I was thing – discreet. All I said was – what about it, Alge? We can let bygones be bygones, can't we?

Darnley   What did he say to that?

Rocco   I tell you, Darnley, your brother was very reasonable.

Darnley   Oh, shit.

Rocco   No, he was!

Darnley   Did he say, 'I'm a reasonable man'?

Rocco   Yes, he did, as a matter of fact.

Darnley   Oh, Christ!

Rocco   Look – I'll be frank. I explained the whole situation – what happened, like. About the money and that.

Darnley   What did you tell him?

Rocco   Well – knowing what a soft spot he has for his mum, like, I said she was responsible.

Darnley   For what?

Rocco   Spending his hard-earned dinero and that. He knows what she's like.

Darnley   Oh, she's going to love that.

Rocco   Well, don't tell her, for Christ's sake! I'm relying on your tact and diplomacy here.

Darnley   What about Algeria?

Rocco   What?

Darnley   His fiancée. The tart you offed.

Rocco   Oh, good as gold, good as gold. Algie understands about business. I mean, I let Emmie off the hook a bit, anyway. Said she was getting confused and that in her old age. Basically, I said it was a series of tragic accidents with your crazed mother at the helm, like. You, I exonerated entirely.

Darnley   Oh, yes?

Rocco   We can do it, Darn! We can get out of here. Back to the Smoke. I got to do it, Darn. I'm wasting my life away here.

Darnley   What, and you really think he'll just do nothing? Let bygones be bygones?

Rocco   His very words, Darn. I mean, I can't guarantee what he might do in regards to your mum, but . . .

Darnley   What about Chrissie?

Rocco   Well, no. I mean someone has to carry the can when all's said and done. She was sort of cast in the role of crazed mum's helper. You don't owe Chrissie nothing, mate! I mean, don't get me wrong but I don't hear any sounds of marital bliss coming out your bedroom these days.

Darnley   Have you been listening?

Rocco   I can't help but bloody listen, can I? Laying here on this settee. I mean, at first I was embarrassed, like. But after a while I didn't hear very much and I said to myself – no, love is dead, I said. The magic is gone from that marriage.

Darnley   All right, all right. No, I can't do it, Rocco. I can't portray Mum and Chrissie.

Rocco   Algie still won't know where they are.

Darnley   He will. He'll get it out of me. He can always get stuff out of me, can Algie. Always could.

Rocco   He wouldn't get nothing out of me.

Darnley   Yeah – but you're not his big brother and living with him and that. You can go, if you want.

Rocco   I can't! Not by myself. How am I going to get down them stairs?

Darnley   That's your problem, mate.

Rocco   Oh, come on, Darn!

Darnley   I'm sorry – no.

Rocco   Oh, Christ! Just give me a hand with the stairs, then.

Darnley   No. I don't want no part of it.

Rocco   I won't grass, Darnley. I swear I won't grass. Would I grass? You know me – my word is my bond.

Darnley   You killed my dad, for fuck's sake.

Rocco   I never took you as being small-minded, Darnley.

Darnley   Oh, Christ! Oh, go on, then. Just the stairs, mind.

Rocco   Oh, Darn! You're a good boy, Darn – I always said. You get back from downstairs at – what? – about one o'clock, yes?

Darnley   Tonight, you mean? Blimey!

Rocco   I don't want to hang about, Darn. We wait until they're asleep – I'll be all dressed and ready.

Darnley   All right. About three o'clock, then? Just to be on the safe side. We don't want to –

The kitchen door opens and **Emmie** *comes in.*

Emmie (*to* **Darnley**)   You still here? Aren't you going to have a kip?

Darnley   Me and Rocco was talking.

Emmie   Oh, I'm sorry I missed that. I left them beans somewhere.

She crosses to the table and starts to look for them.

Darnley   No, I was just telling Rocco – I've been talking to Eduardo about Chrissie joining Los Cubanos.

Emmie   Oh, fucking wonderful!

Darnley   What?

Emmie   She'll be fucking thrilled about that. There they are!

She has found the packet of beans on the floor by the table.

Darnley   She will! She hates just waiting at tables.

Emmie   So you make her sing and all!

Darnley   No – but she'll love that! It's artistic. It's showbiz. And she'll get extra money. We could go independent. You know, her and me. Doing clubs and that. I even thought of a name – Los Dos Inglesas.

Emmie   Los Dos Cuntos.

Darnley   Oh – you're always down on anything new. You want to get with it, Ma.

Emmie   You listen to me, my son. I wasn't born with it, I never bought it and I hope I go to my grave without it. Now then.

Darnley   Anyway, I'm going to have a lay down till supper. Give us a shout when Chrissie gets back.

He opens the door that **Rocco** *came out of and goes in, closing it behind him.*

Emmie (*to* **Rocco**)   I sometimes wonder, I really do! How did I manage to produce that? Course, Chrissie's dad wasn't the sharpest shovel in the shed, I don't suppose. You never knew Chrissie's dad, did you?

Rocco *doesn't reply and* **Emmie** *realises he's fast asleep.*

Emmie   Talking to my bloody self again!

As she does so, the entryphone buzzes. **Emmie** *freezes, staring at the entryphone. It buzzes again.* **Emmie** *slowly puts the beans back on the table and walks to the entryphone. She lifts the receiver nervously, but doesn't speak.* **Chrissie***'s distorted voice comes over the loudspeaker.*

Chrissie (*offstage*)   Hello? Hello? Emmie?

Emmie (*recovering*)   Chrissie?

Chrissie (*offstage*)   Let me in, will you? I ain't got my key.

Emmie   Oh. I'll open the door.

She presses the button, replaces the receiver, goes to the front door and opens it. She looks down the stairs.

You all right, girl?

Chrissie *comes in.*

Chrissie   Oh, those fucking stairs!

She goes straight to the sofa and collapses on to it.

Emmie *is in a state of high expectancy.*

Emmie   Well?

Chrissie   Jesus fucking shite!

She glances at **Rocco** *at the other end of the sofa.*

Chrissie   Is he kipping again?

Emmie   How'd it go?

Chrissie   I'm done in.

Emmie   How'd you get on?

Chrissie   Oh . . .

Emmie   Oh, come on Chrissie, for fuck's sake! What did he say?

Chrissie   I never saw him, did I?

Emmie (*dismayed*)   You never saw him!

Chrissie   Never turned up.

Emmie   He never turned up?

Chrissie (*irritably*)   He never fucking turned up!

Emmie   All right, all right! That's not like Algie, though. Not when he said he would.

Chrissie   Well, he didn't.

Emmie   Oh, Chrissie! Are you sure you went to the right place?

Chrissie   Course I did!

Emmie   Something must of happened to him. Did you try his mobile?

Chrissie   It were switched off.

Emmie   Something's happened to him! He ain't never had that mobile switched off since the day they was invented.

Chrissie   So . . . Well, that's it, I suppose.

Emmie   It can't be, Chrissie! I can't go on in this place. It's a living death, Chrissie – a living death.

Chrissie   I know.

Emmie   I been excited all day, thinking about it.

Chrissie   Yeah – well.

Emmie *is suddenly suspicious.*

Emmie   You're taking this very calm.

Chrissie   No, I'm not.

Emmie   Very calm.

Chrissie   No! I'm ever so upset.

Emmie   You don't look it.

Chrissie   You should of seen me earlier – Oh . . . !

Emmie   What?

Chrissie   I was upset then.

Emmie   What did you do?

Chrissie   What?

Emmie   When you was upset.

Chrissie   Oh . . . You know – crying . . . My mascara was all down my face . . .

Emmie   Was it?

Chrissie   Well, I've put on new now. What did I look like, though? In the caff, it was, too. You know – the caff where we was suppose to meet. Everyone looking at me . . .

Emmie   Oh, dear. Only I'd hate to think you was trying to stitch me up, Chrissie.

Chrissie   Stitch you up?

Emmie   I'd really hate that.

Chrissie   How would I stitch you up?

Emmie   Like if you'd done some deal with Algie to hand me over and you get off Scotch free.

Chrissie *gets to her feet and faces* **Emmie**.

Chrissie   I'm going to get really annoyed in a minute. I am!

Emmie   Oh, well, I wouldn't want that, Chrissie.

Chrissie   No, well . . .

Emmie   Seeing as I'm not a violent person. I mean, I can't remember the last time I cut someone. Not seriously. Little

Kerry Titchmarsh, was it? No. No, she was up and about again in a week.

Chrissie   She was well out of order, Emmie. Making remarks.

Emmie   Only, I mean, I can't help wondering, you see, what the fuck you're doing wearing that new dress which ain't the one you left the house in this morning.

Chrissie *looks at her for a long moment, then suddenly laughs.*

Chrissie   You should see your face!

She doubles over with laughter. **Emmie** *looks on, stony-faced.*

Chrissie   Oh, dear!

She wipes a tear from her eye.

Emmie   Let's all have a share of the joke, Chrissie, eh?

Chrissie   I was winding you up, wasn't I?

Emmie   Was you?

Chrissie   Course I was! You don't think I'd . . . ? Oh, Emmie! Algie said you'd take it serious.

Emmie   Algie said? So you did see him?

Chrissie   Course I did! It were his idea. Wind the old cow up, he said.

Emmie   Aah! Little rascal!

Chrissie   It was him bought the dress for me.

Emmie   No! Isn't that just like him, though?

Chrissie   What do you think?

She twirls round, showing off the dress.

Emmie   Oh, it's lovely, Chrissie! So it went all right, did it?

Chrissie   I'm here, ain't I?

Emmie   Well, tell me! Tell me!

Chrissie   Where's droopy-drawers?

Emmie   Oh, he's having a lay down. What happened? He wasn't half surprised, I bet!

Chrissie   He never let on if he was.

Emmie   Oh – Mr Cool!

Chrissie   He did reckon we was abroad, though.

Emmie   Fat fucking chance! You didn't tell him we were in Luton?

Chrissie   Course not! I didn't tell him nothing. Said I'd just flown over for the day, like.

Emmie   He could of followed you back.

Chrissie   Nah!

Emmie   It's not that I don't like trust him, but he's a treacherous little bastard, bless him.

Chrissie   Algie's changed, Emmie. I think tragedy has left its mark on him. He's a reasonable man, Emmie. He said so himself.

Emmie   Did he? What about the money?

Chrissie   Easy come, easy go, he says.

Emmie   Easy come, easy go?

Chrissie   That's what he says. He were a bit sad, like.

Emmie   What about the girl, though – what was her name?

Chrissie   Oh, I don't know – Niagara or something.

Emmie   But he's all right about her?

Chrissie   Oh, yes! I explained it to him, see? Told him what happened. I mean, basically the bottom line is, he blames Darnley.

Emmie   Does he?

Chrissie   What he says is, Darnley was meant to be the man of the house while he were away.

Emmie   That's true, I suppose.

Chrissie   He should of stopped us.

Emmie   He should of. I remember thinking that at the time.

Chrissie   He should of shown us a lead – where we was going wrong, like.

Emmie   It's true. So what's he going to do?

Chrissie   Well – we can go back to London!

Emmie   Oh, Chrissie!

Chrissie   Back to the shops! Proper food! Friendly faces!

Emmie   Oh, Chrissie! I don't think I could of lasted another year in Luton. I am worried about this business with Darnley, though.

Chrissie   What business?

Emmie   Well, I mean, what's Algie going to do, like?

Chrissie   Well, Darnley has sort of transgressed the unwritten law, hasn't he?

Emmie   Well – yes.

Chrissie   Well, it's up to Algie then, innit?

Emmie   I mean, do you think he'll . . . ?

Chrissie   He don't have no choice, Emmie.

Emmie   No, I suppose not. But I hate to see one brother set against another, like. It's like something out the Bible, innit?

Chrissie   Is it?

Emmie   Chrissie – I wouldn't like mention any of this to Darnley.

Chrissie   He's only got hisself to blame. He's got to face it some time. I've had enough deceit.

Emmie   Oh, I know. Me, too. But he can face it after we've gone, though. We can leave him a little note. It'll be kindest that way. I mean, tomorrow we can just like slip off back to London . . .

Chrissie   And let nature take its course.

Emmie   There's nothing we can do, is there?

Chrissie   We shouldn't meddle. We'd only complicate things.

Emmie   Algie wouldn't thank us for that.

Chrissie   He certainly fucking wouldn't! And listen – guess what!

Emmie   What?

Chrissie   Algie's got this job lined up for me. On television!

Emmie   No!

Chrissie   He's got to know this big TV producer – got his own company for producing things. They was on the same landing in Pentonville. Algie's got this one last big job to do – him and this TV man – and then they're going straight.

Emmie   What's this job he's got for you, though?

Chrissie   Well – they're going to start me off just reading the news, like, then they'll move me up to doing my own quiz show.

Emmie   Oh, Chrissie!

Chrissie   It's going to be called *Arse No Questions*.

Emmie   It's a good name.

Chrissie   They show you these big photographs of celebrities' arses and you have to guess whose they are.

Emmie   That's brilliant!

Chrissie   I'll be in charge, like. I'll be dressed in a sort of mortar board and one of them sort of little black dress things they wear and stockings and I'll point at the arses with a stick.

Emmie   It's a brilliant name – *Arse No Questions*. It's like 'Ask No Questions'.

Chrissie   Oh, yeah! Hey! Brilliant, innit? And the prizes they're going to have!

Emmie   What?

Chrissie   Oh, I dunno. Depends how many arses you get right. But big prizes – holidays in exotic locations – fitted dining suites – luxury cars . . . And if they don't get any right, they have to bend over and I like beat them with the stick I've got for pointing. Only, only pretend, I suppose.

Emmie   Oh, Chrissie! I always knew you'd make it.

She takes **Chrissie** *in her arms and hugs her.*

Emmie   There'll be no holding you back now. Out every night, you'll be, in these restaurants, sipping champagne, waving at Posh and Becks . . .

She starts to cry.

Chrissie (*comforting her*)   Hey! Well, one step at a time, eh?

Emmie   You'll have your star on Sunset Boulevard, I bet!

Darnley *appears in the bedroom doorway.*

Darnley   What's going on?

Chrissie   What do you mean?

Darnley   You all right, Mum?

Chrissie   She's all right.

Emmie   I'm all right. Got something in my eye. Here, look at the time! I better get these beans done.

She bustles over to the table.

Darnley (*to* **Chrissie**)   Eduardo was really pissed off with you.

Chrissie   Well, fuck him!

Emmie   And the horse he rode in on!

Darnley   Where was you?

Chrissie   I told you!

Darnley   Look – you got to pull your socks up, Chrissie.

Chrissie   Oh, yes?

Darnley   I've been talking to Eduardo about us.

Chrissie   What do you mean, about us?

Darnley   About us! About working at El Mondo Mexicano. Only doing something different, like.

Chrissie   Oh, be still, my heart!

Emmie   No, you want to listen to this, Chrissie.

Chrissie   Go on then.

Darnley   Well, Eduardo says, if you're on time for the next few weeks, and don't go upsetting the customers and that –

Chrissie   Excuse me! I did not upset his poncey fucking customers!

Darnley   Well – be that as it may –

Chrissie   Never you mind about be that as it may – you just listen to me, Darnley Packer. The people who come into Eduardo's fucking club are nothing but Luton low-lifes and low-lifes don't come no lower than Luton fucking low-lifes. And if one of his cunting no-neck friends puts his hand up my fucking skirt and I just happen to like accidentally empty a litre of his poncey fucking sangria over his scabby head that's just Eduardo's tough shit.

Darnley   All right, all right. There was faults on both sides, I grant you.

Chrissie   No there wasn't!

Darnley   Will you listen!

Chrissie   No, I fucking won't!

Emmie   Listen to him, Chrissie – go on.

Chrissie   Oh . . .

Darnley   Come on, love – this could be a big break for us.

Chrissie   What could?

Darnley   That's what I'm trying to tell you. Eduardo's willing to give you a chance to join El Cubanos.

Chrissie *stares at him for a long moment.*

Chrissie   And?

Darnley   So it won't be just us three guys – it'll be three guys and a gal!

Chrissie   And this is my big break, is it?

Emmie (*warningly*)   Chrissie! I think it sounds nice. (*To* **Darnley**.) Tell her the other bit.

Darnley   Well, what I thought was, we – that's you and me, like we might sort of use this as a springboard for our double act.

Chrissie   Our what?

Darnley   Los Dos Inglesas. It means The Two English. We cut out Arnold and Kevin and go off on our own, like. There's pubs and clubs crying out for an act like that. I mean, a good-looking couple like us performing Latin American hits – where could we go wrong? And – who knows? – maybe a season at a holiday camp. The world's our whatsit! What do you think?

Chrissie *just stares at* **Darnley**, *unable to speak.*

Darnley   There – I told you! She's always saying I never think about our future.

Chrissie *takes a deep breath.*

Chrissie   You really want to know what I think?

Emmie (*hastily*)   He's right, Chrissie – you have to think about *tomorrow*!

Darnley   First thing, though, we've got to get you ready for the audition.

Chrissie   What do you mean?

Darnley   Eduardo can't be expected to take you on sight unseen, can he?

Chrissie   He's seen me!

Emmie   I'll go and get on with the supper.

She hurries out, taking the beans with her.

Darnley   I got this backing tape from downstairs we can use.

He puts a tape into the cassette player.

First thing, though, is the maracas.

Chrissie   The maracas, yes.

Darnley *goes to the sofa and picks up the maracas. He notices* **Rocco**.

Darnley   Blimey, is he asleep again? Now, the basic rhythm is boom-chick-a, boom-chick-a, boom-chick-a, boom-chick. It's quite simple.

He demonstrates.

See?

He puts the maracas in her hands.

Now you have a go.

Chrissie   Do I have to do this?

Darnley   Have a go – go on!

Chrissie *tries to play the maracas. She doesn't do it very well.*

Chrissie   I can't do this.

Darnley   Try saying it at the same time. That may be a help.

Chrissie   Boom-chick, boom-chick, boom-chick.

Darnley   No, no, no – where you're going wrong is, you're missing the 'er'.

Chrissie   'Er'?

Darnley   Boom-chick-*a*, boom-chick-*a*, boom-chick-*a*, boom-chick.

Chrissie   Oh, the 'er'! I'm not going to do this.

Darnley   Course you are.

Chrissie   I'm not going to stand up on some stage saying boom-chick, boom-chick.

Darnley   Not boom-chick, boom-chick . . .

Chrissie   I don't give a flying fuck what it is – I'm not fucking doing it!

Darnley   All right, all right. Calm down. We'll leave the maracas for now. I thought you'd like them. Boom-chick-a, boom-chick-a, boom-chick-a, boom-chick.

Chrissie   Waving some fucking baby's rattle about . . .

Darnley   All right. We'll do the song then.

Chrissie   Oh, fucking hell!

Darnley   I'll do the first verse, then take you through it.

He switches on the tape, waits while it plays a few bars of introduction, then launches into the song. 'I, Yi, Yi, Yi, Yi (I Like You Very Much)'.[1]

He switches off the tape.

All right?

---

[1] From the film *That Night in Rio*, lyrics by Mack Gordon and music by Harry Warren, Twentieth Century Music Corporation, 1942.

Chrissie *stands looking at him, stunned.*

Darnley   Okay. First line. 'I yi yi yi yi, I like you very much.' Now you.

Chrissie   Where did you find this?

Darnley   I didn't have to find it. It's a Carmen Miranda classic.

Chrissie   Well, he's welcome to it.

Darnley   From the film *That Night in Rio*. 1941. Come on, 'I yi yi yi yi, I like you very much.'

Chrissie   'I yi yi yi yi, I like you very much.'

Darnley   Don't just say it! You're meant to sing it!

Chrissie   I don't want to sing it! It's horrible!

Darnley   It's not horrible! It's nice! It's sexy!

Chrissie   Sexy?

Darnley   Listen – I'll just sing the bridge and the last verse. You'll like those.

He sings, ogling **Chrissie** *and exaggerating the flirtatiousness of the lyric horribly.*

Chrissie   I feel ill.

Darnley   What do you mean?

Chrissie   You make me feel fucking ill, that's what I fucking mean! If you think I'm going to waste the rest of my life traipsing round fucking boozers with you making an exhibition of yourself, you're even more of a prat than you look!

She storms off into the kitchen.

Darnley   Chrissie!

Rocco   You want to watch yourself, son.

Darnley *whirls round, surprised.*

Darnley   Oh shut up, for fuck's sake!

Rocco   All right. All right.

Darnley   What do you mean, 'all right, all right'?

Rocco   Just don't come to me saying I didn't warn you, that's all.

Darnley   Warn me about what?

Rocco   No. No, you don't want to hear.

Darnley   Yes, I do.

Rocco   No you don't.

Darnley   Oh, shut the fuck up, then!

Rocco   She's going to dump you.

Darnley   What do you mean, dump me?

Rocco   Dump as in dump. You as in you.

Darnley   Wait a minute, wait a minute! Who's going to dump me?

Rocco   Her. And your mother.

Darnley   You're like some slimy old lizard, you are.

Rocco   Oh, that's nice!

Darnley   How can Chrissie – my wife – how can she dump me? Eh?

Rocco   She's been to see Algie.

Darnley *stares at him.*

Darnley   You've lost your marbles, you have.

Rocco *gets to his feet and reaches for his walking frame.*

Rocco   Oh, well . . .

Darnley   You come up with these fantastic ideas . . .

Rocco   I heard them talking. They thought I was asleep.

Darnley   Talking about what?

Rocco   Algie. How she's been to see him.

Darnley   Get away! You amaze me, you do. You lie about here all day like some Persian fucking prince and you dream up these stupid ideas all the time. You're not helping yourself, you know. People get pissed off with people like you. Serve you right if I didn't help you with them stairs tonight.

Rocco (*furiously*)   I never wanted to be here, did I? I had my nice little house, my hobbies, my garden . . .

Darnley   Garden! You covered it in concrete.

Rocco   That's the finest moss-resistant, reconstituted York stone, that is. As used in York Cathedral by craftsmen of old. Guaranteed for five hundred years. I've always had this sort of idea. In a thousand years or so that *Time Team* or someone will come digging, and they'll find my little house and they'll find my porcelain shoes and my collection of German militaria – oh, and my almost-life-size statue of Snow White and the Four Dwarves – the company went bust before it finished the set . . . Anyway, they'll dig all this up piece by piece and the little nasty one will say, 'This was obviously the house of a warrior, but a warrior who loved the good things of life.'

Darnley   They saw you coming, mate.

Rocco   You just don't want to hear the truth, do you? They're leaving tomorrow.

Darnley   Bollocks. You're getting all confused. It's you that's leaving.

Rocco   They're going to leave you a note. She's seen Algie. She's blamed you about the money and that girl I offed for you. And Algie's said they can go back, no hard feelings and he can see it was all your fault.

Darnley   How can it be my fault when they go and spend all his money? How can it be my fault when Mum decides she's going to get you to kill his girl?

Rocco   Don't ask me, mate.

Darnley   You see? It don't make sense.

Rocco   It's what Algie believes, though – since your darling wife got at him. He bought her that new dress she's wearing!

Darnley   What dress?

Rocco   She's wearing a new dress.

Darnley   No, she's not.

Rocco   God blimey! She's wearing a new dress! Algie bought it for her, she says.

Darnley   Bollocks! Why would Algie buy her a dress?

Rocco   How should I know? Ask her! Ask her yourself!

Darnley   What, just turn round and say, did Algie buy you that dress?

Rocco   Why not?

Darnley   Because she'll think I've gone barmy, that's why not.

He stares, undecided, at **Rocco** *for a moment, then strides to the kitchen door and opens it.*

Darnley   Chrissie?

Chrissie (*offstage*)   What?

Darnley   Come in here a minute, will you?

Chrissie (*offstage*)   Fuck off!

Darnley   No, I want to ask you something.

Chrissie (*offstage*)   Fuck off!

From the kitchen we half hear **Emmie** *saying something to* **Chrissie**.

Darnley *stands aside for* **Chrissie** *to flounce into the room.*

Chrissie   It's nothing to do with that fucking chicka-chicka business, is it?

Darnley   You're looking nice this evening.

Chrissie   What's your game?

Darnley   No, I'm just saying.

Chrissie   Well, you can fuck off, then.

She starts back towards the kitchen.

Darnley   New dress, is it?

Chrissie *stops dead and slowly turns back to face* **Darnley**.

Chrissie   What if it is?

Darnley   I wondered if someone might of bought it for you.

Chrissie *looks slowly from* **Darnley** *to* **Rocco** *and back again, then walks to the front door and opens it wide. The two men watch her, puzzled.*

Chrissie *comes back, grabs hold of* **Rocco** *and starts to stumble him towards the door.*

Rocco   Here!

Chrissie   You're going for a little walk, Rocco.

Rocco   I can't. I can't do the stairs.

He starts to resist, but **Chrissie** *is too strong for him.*

Rocco   Here!

Darnley   What are you doing?

Chrissie   Come on, Rocco – you can do it. Go on!

She is heaving on one of **Rocco**'s *arms.* **Darnley** *now grabs the other and pulls in the opposite direction.*

Darnley   You can't do that! You'll kill him!

Chrissie   You grassed me up, Rocco! You pay the fucking penalty!

Rocco   Ow! Leave off! Ow!

Darnley   Let him alone!

Darnley *stumbles and loses his grip.*

Chrissie   You go down there, you cunt, where you belong. Down you go!

She gives a final heave and we hear **Rocco** *crash from step to step down the stairs. Then silence.*

Darnley *goes to the door and looks down the stairs.*

Darnley   You've killed him!

Chrissie   He fell down the stairs.

Darnley   Nobody's going to believe that! He couldn't walk without his Zimmer.

Chrissie *crosses the room, picks up the Zimmer frame and takes it back to the door. She hurls it after* **Rocco**, *then shuts the door and turns to face* **Darnley**.

Chrissie   There!

Darnley   So he was right.

Chrissie   He were a grass.

Darnley   You did see Algie.

Chrissie (*mimicking him*)   'You did see Algie'.

Darnley   Well, did you?

Chrissie   What if I did? What are you going to do about it?

Darnley   I just want to know.

Chrissie   I bet you do!

She starts to walk past him towards the kitchen. He grabs her arm. She pulls away and turns to face him, furious.

Don't you touch me, you wanker! I'm going to be a fucking
star with Algie. Out clubbing every night, I'll be – and not
down El Mondo Mexicano, neither! I'll be driven about in
limos and wear clothes you can see through and have my
picture in the papers being nice to a lot of starving black
kiddies with flies all over them. Everybody'll want my opinion
on like world affairs – global warning and that and whether
I'm having it off with Robbie Williams. I won't have cunts like
you touching me, even. They'll have to treat me with fucking
respect.

Darnley   What did you say to him?

Chrissie   I told him the truth. I told him Emmie and me
wanted to go back to London and we was very sorry and it was
all your fault what we done.

Darnley   How was it my fault?

Chrissie   Because you're a chicken-shit, limp-dick big girl's
blouse and you're not half the man Algie is.

Darnley   You told him that, did you?

Chrissie   He didn't need telling. Why do you think I
married you?

Darnley   For what you could get out of me.

Chrissie   Get out of you? If you was a tube of Dairylea I
couldn't squeeze cheese out of you. I married you because it
was the only way I could get near Algie.

Darnley   Lying cow! Lying fucking cow!

Chrissie   Why would I marry you? You was a joke with
your brothel-creepers and your hair your mother used to cut.

Darnley   Why didn't you just marry him, then?

Chrissie   I could of.

The truth dawns on **Darnley**.

Darnley   He wouldn't have you!

Chrissie   None of your fucking business!

Darnley   He wouldn't have you, would he?

Chrissie   He'd have me all right – he never stopped having me! But he said why should I get married when I can have all the fun and none of the responsibility? I ditched him after that, but then he started up again after we was married so . . .

She shrugs.

Anyway, I'm out of here. I'm going to get packed.

She goes towards the bedroom.

Darnley   Wait a minute! Wait a minute!

Chrissie   Get a fucking life, Darnley.

Darnley   Chrissie!

She goes. **Darnley** *stands staring after her for a long moment, then he slowly goes to the table and opens a drawer. He scrabbles around in the contents for a moment, then finds what he is looking for – the revolver. He checks that it is loaded and goes towards the bedroom after* **Chrissie***. He goes in, closing the door after him.*

The revolver fires three times. Two seconds later **Emmie** *comes out of the kitchen like a greyhound out of the traps. She wrenches open the drawer and desperately starts looking for the revolver.*

She is still looking when **Darnley** *comes back into the room, the gun still in his hand.*

Darnley   She's gone.

Emmie *nearly jumps out of her skin.*

Emmie   Oh! Oh, you did give me a start. I was just looking for the gravy fork.

Darnley   I shot her.

Emmie *laughs.*

Darnley   She's dead.

Emmie   Well – can't be helped, I suppose.

She is sidling towards the front door.

She was never what I call robust, was she? She was always a very spiritual person.

Darnley   Spiritual?

Emmie   Yeah – you know – sort of sickly.

Darnley   No, she wasn't.

Emmie   No? Oh, well maybe not. I mean, you should know her better than me.

Darnley   I didn't, though, did I? I thought that woman adored me.

Emmie   She did! She did! Well – in her way she did. I'd better get on with the dinner.

Darnley   The kitchen's that way.

He points helpfully.

Emmie   Oh – course it is! What am I like, eh?

Darnley   You wouldn't be able to get out that way, anyway. Not without treading on Rocco. Mind you, you wouldn't be able to open the door, anyway, with him there. He's like wedged between the bottom of the stairs and the front door.

Emmie   What's – I mean, what's he lying there for?

Darnley   He's dead, too.

Emmie   Blimey – you've been having a bit of a time, haven't you?

Darnley   I didn't do it. Chrissie threw him down the stairs.

Emmie   Oh. Well – he was old.

Darnley   She said the only reason she married me was to get near Algie.

Emmie (*laughing*)   No! She's just teasing! Winding you up, like.

Darnley   No she wasn't. She was having it away with Algie from day one. What's wrong with this family?

Emmie   Oh – all families have their little ways, son.

Darnley   Little ways? It's like some bleeding circus! My wife's screwing my brother, my mother's been having it off with my father-in-law, my brother hired a hit man to kill my father and I'm married to my sister! This can't be right.

Emmie   Who are we to judge?

Darnley   You got to have some rules like, haven't you?

Emmie   What are you? One of these fucking puritans? Thou shalt not do this and wilt not do that and you'd better not try the other? Some sort of creeping Jesus? It's all very fine and large, this stuff in the Bible, but what a fucking waste of time! Do unto others before they do you, mate – that's the only commandment you need. I can't be doing with all these so-called morals. Ruin your fucking life, they do.

Darnley   You can't just –

Emmie   Feelings is what counts! Feelings! If you feel inside here it's right, that's all the morals you need.

Darnley   Well, I feel it, Mum, I really feel it.

He shoots her.

Emmie   Oh! Oh, Darnley! There's no call for that, Darnley.

He shoots again. **Emmie** *falls to her knees. She puts her hand to her stomach, then looks at the blood on it.*

Emmie   Now look what you done!

Darnley *shoots again.*

Emmie (*reproachfully*)   Oh, Darnley!

She falls to the floor, dead. **Darnley** *stands looking down at her.*

The entryphone buzzes. **Darnley** *doesn't move.*

It buzzes again. **Darnley** *looks at it and slowly walks across and lifts the receiver.*

Darnley   Yes?

Algie (*offstage*)   Hello, Darn. It's your little brother.

Curtain.